TEDDY BEARS

TEDDY BEARS

A Complete Guide to History, Collecting, and Care

Sue Pearson and Dottie Ayers

MACMILLAN • USA

This book is dedicated to the Agg children,
Edward, William, Thomas, Henry, and Emily

Macmillan
A Simon & Schuster Macmillan Company
1633 Broadway
New York, NY 10019

Created by De Agostini Editions Ltd., London,
England

Copyright © De Agostini Editions Ltd. 1995
Text © Sue Pearson 1995

Library of Congress Cataloging-in-Publication Data

Pearson, Sue
   Teddy Bears : a complete guide to their history,
collecting, and care / by Sue Pearson and Dottie Ayers.
     p. cm.
   Includes bibliographical references and index.
   ISBN 0-02-860417-2 (cloth)
   1. Teddy Bears—Collectors and collecting. I. Ayers,
Dottie. II. Title.
   NK8740.P43 1995
   688.7'24—dc20   95-11517
                                          CIP

Printed in Italy by Officine Grafiche De Agostini,
Novara

10 9 8 7 6 5 4 3 2 1

Contents

Introduction *by Sue Pearson*

Collecting teddy bears has brought me a great deal of pleasure. It has taken me to many countries, and through bears I have met some wonderful people and made a lot of dear friends. I fell in love with the first bear I ever had, given to me in my early years by my mother. He had belonged to her as a child and came to me wearing a beautiful silver-buttoned waistcoat made by my grandmother. I still have him today, and he enjoys pride of place in my collection.

I am extremely lucky that in my little shop in the historic Lanes in Brighton I get to see some wonderful bears. My shop is bulging with them, and it is a constant source of delight to me when I open for business in the morning to see all those charming furry faces looking at me. Of course I keep some because, just like any other collector, there is is always that special bear that says "take me home," and I just can't resist. I am happy to be able to share some of my bears with you in this book, and hope they inspire you to go out and find your own, because I know it can only be a happy experience.

LEFT A picture of myself with just a few of my favorite bears.

RIGHT My very first bear, given to me by my mother when I was a child.

Starting a Bear Collection

Bear hunt

How people collect bears is always a matter of personal taste —if you were to put ten collectors in a room together and give them a group of bears to choose from, they would probably all pick something different.

Some collectors like only new bears, either made by one of the many teddy bear artists producing bears today, or by one of the famous manufacturers still making bears, such as Steiff and Gebrüder Hermann in Germany, and Merrythought and Dean's in England. But others will only collect bears from before the Second World War. People often start off by buying just one particular type of bear, such as the replicas of a certain manufacturer or the bears of one bear artist. Although this is a good way to begin, it limits the choice, and most collectors soon move on to extend their collection into other areas.

A 1991 Merry-thought bear

Collecting bears by color can be very rewarding—black bears are particularly sought-after. Although this of course limits the choice considerably, it can provide quite a challenge for the bear hunter. Collecting bears in different colors offers the collector a wider variety. A collection of colored bears makes an attractive display. Bears were produced in the late 1920s and during the 1930s in a wide variety of colors and in several different combinations—pink, blue, green, purple, orange, and white are just some of the bear colors you can find.

Red, white and blue miniature mascot bears from the First World War

People like to collect miniatures because they take up little room. This is important if you have limited space—it is amazing how quickly bears can spread and take over a house! There is a great choice of miniatures available because they were not only made by the major early manufacturers, such as Schuco and Steiff, but are also still being made by bear artists and modern manufacturers. They are often brightly colored and many are novelty examples, which look very pretty when displayed together in a glass cabinet.

While some collectors of vintage bears may buy bears only in perfect, unrestored condition, others search for battered old bears they feel have a special charm. Similarly, some people insist on having documentation for their bears and will only buy bears by named makers and with their labels. But bears by unidentified makers can form an interesting collection, and sometimes for a lower price.

LEFT A German musical bear by Jopi from the 1920s

RIGHT A multi-colored Chiltern Hugmee bear from the 1930s

Dressed bears are also popular. You can buy vintage and modern dressed bears, as well as miniature ones. Many bear artists also dress their bears. However, for some collectors, only bears in their "natural" state are worth collecting, and the quality and condition of the mohair becomes paramount.

Many bears have interesting histories and may be accompanied by photographs with their original owner, and a family history. Although difficult to build up a whole collection of such bears, one or two enhance any collection.

But these are only suggestions. Don't feel you have to collect bears by a particular type—there are hundreds more collectors who collect any bear, old or new, small or large, the only criterion being that they fall in love with a bear and have to take him home.

Although in a poor state, this bear has an appealing face

So who collects bears? A bear given as a childhood present, or a vintage bear inherited from a relative has inspired many a collector. Other collectors have been moved to buy a bear as a companion to one they have just found in their attic or an old cupboard.

Bears have always been associated with romance—given to loved ones for birthdays and special events—and these too may start off a collection. Bears are collected by both men and women, young and old, and sometimes couples have even fallen out because they couldn't agree when trying to choose a bear!

Where you go to buy your bear is very much determined by where you live; in some countries collectors' bears are much more widely available than in others, and avid collectors may even decide to travel abroad to furnish their collection. Those who are

Twin bears from c.1912 dressed in old christening gowns

lucky enough to have a specialist teddy bear store in their area can browse at leisure, and often enlist the help of the staff when trying to make a purchase. In addition, stores will provide you with a proper receipt giving the approximate date the bear was made, and the maker if known (which is helpful when trying to insure your bears). Many stores will allow you to pay for a bear in installments, which is useful for those on a limited budget.

For those who do not have a retailer near them, it is possible to subscribe to one of the excellent teddy bear magazines published throughout the world. These have articles about bears and are filled with ads from suppliers, many of which operate a mail order service.

Teddy bear fairs provide the perfect marketplace for the collector. They are held worldwide, and are listed in teddy

LEFT These two lovely old Steiffs were owned by twin girls

LEFT Bears accompanied by photographs of themselves with their original owner are always popular with collectors

bear magazines and directories. At the fair you will find teddy bear artists, dealers, and stores all under one roof. Having so many bears together is particularly useful in providing the beginner with an idea of the variety of bears on the market, and their prices. There are usually experts on hand to give advice and handy tips, so don't be afraid to ask.

For people with a more limited budget, garage sales and flea markets often have bargains. Bears can also turn up in auctions of furniture and household items, sitting forlornly all alone hoping someone will give them a good home. The larger auction houses throughout the world have special sales devoted to teddy bears and dolls, and it is here that you may just find the one bear you are looking for.

The essential purchase for any serious teddy bear collector is a book on the subject, available through your local bookstore or by mail order. This will provide you with useful background reading, and should point you in the right direction. Before buying a bear it is a good idea to begin by browsing—visit bear stores and wherever possible get close to

Unidentified bears can be lovely, and are also relatively inexpensive

the bears so that you can get the feel of them and recognize the different materials used. And remember, your tastes may change, so spending time discovering your likes and dislikes should prevent you from making some hasty purchases.

Documentation

Wherever you buy a bear, whether it is at a store or an auction house, always get a receipt giving the approximate date (the most important thing—particularly if it is before 1940) and, if known, the maker and country of origin. And it is essential to get any bear of value insured. Take a photograph of your bear and keep it with the insurance documents.

Fakes

Because of the popularity of old bears there are now a lot of fakes on the market. It can be very disappointing for a collector to find that the dirty old bear bought at an antique fair for a high price is a fake, and, unfortunately, without a receipt nothing can be done. Fake bears have been produced deliberately to deceive. They should not be confused with new artist bears or replicas that have labels on them, which, although based on traditional vintage designs, are not pretending to be old. Luckily, fakes are quite distinctive, deliberately incorporating many of the elements associated with old

A typical fake

bears (long arms, hump, straw stuffing), although not usually in the right combinations, and once you have seen one, hopefully you should be able to identify them all. Perhaps one of the most distinguishing characteristics of fakes is that they are often suspiciously dirty (and may even be deliberately worn on the snout and around the squeaker to make them look even more authentic).

How to use this book and the price guide

Bears in this book are listed geographically and then by maker. There are useful sections on how to look after your bear, and at the back there is a gazetteer giving addresses throughout the world. Important fairs are also listed. The prices are intended as a guide only and represent the current market value at the time the book went to press. They can vary from country to country, and ultimately collectors must really decide the value for themselves. Condition will affect the value greatly—a bear in mint condition with all its labels on will be worth a great deal more than one in only fair condition without its labels. Availability also affects the price, with those most difficult to find commanding a premium.

Bear detective

There are a numer of guidelines you should follow before buying your bear, because sometimes the lovely teddy you have in your hands may not be all he appears to be!

A bear purchaser's checklist

 What fabric has been used? Vintage bears are usually made from wool mohair. Artificial silk plush was used from around 1930, and cotton plush was used after the Second World War. Nylon plush and other synthetic fabrics were introduced in the 1950s. France in particular used short mohair or cotton plush for most of its bears. It is a good idea to get to know the texture and appearance of these different fabrics by looking at and feeling as many bears as you can. Being able to recognize fabric will be very useful when you are trying to date and identify any bear you are thinking of buying.

 Are the ears in the correct position? Check your bear against similar bears in old ads to see if the ears are original. Look to see if there are any holes in the seam of the bear's head where the original ears have been removed. If there are, the ears are likely to be replacements.

 Are the eyes right for the type of bear? If the bear was made before the First World War he should have boot-button eyes. Glass was widely used from the 1920s (although a little earlier in Britain) and plastic from the 1950s.

 Has the nose stitching been replaced, and if it has, is it close to the original? This is very important to assess because each manufacturer tended to have its own distinct nose stitching, making this a good way to identify a bear. Often noses have been replaced with black wool, which is not correct: noses were usually woven from silk thread (although in the 1950s and 1960s rubber and plastic noses were also used).

 What stuffing has been used? Feel the weight of the bear. If he is light, the stuffing is kapok, with some wood wool added if he was made in England. If he is stuffed with only wood wool he will feel crunchy. Bears made after 1940 may have been stuffed with sub-stuffing, and later on very lightweight foam was introduced. In France, excelsior was used later than in Germany and England, and most early French bears are hard-stuffed.

 What are the paw pads made of? Have they been replaced? The most common material for the pads of vintage bears was felt. Cotton was also used, particularly in Australia, but this does not wear well, and will usually have been replaced by now. Velvet and rexine were popular with manufacturers in the late 1930s, and some later bears have pads of plush or leather. In the 1970s a new material, Ultrasuede, was introduced. Although it is always nice if your bear has managed to retain all his original features, paw pads are very susceptible to wear, and as long as they have been replaced sympathetically this will not detract from the value. You may be lucky—in some cases, a new pad may be covering a perfect original.

 Does the bear have a label? This is obviously the easiest and most fail-safe way to identify your bear, but unfortunately many of the earlier bears in particular only had flimsy paper tags, and these are now usually missing. Look for embroidered labels, and metal tags in the ear and on the arm, too.

 Is the bear jointed? Most old bears have round cardboard joints that are not visible, but during the 1960s some bears were unjointed. In France and Japan external joints were preferred, and in Australia, most bears were made without a jointed neck.

 What does the bear look like? Longer arms and a longer muzzle generally mean the bear was made at the beginning of the 20th century. If your bear has a hump, he is probably also vintage. As a general rule, bears after the Second World War tend to have shorter arms and flatter faces. Familiarize yourself with different manufacturers, because often they produced their own distinctive shapes.

 What is the condition of the bear? Look carefully to make sure no damage has been cleverly concealed. If the bear is dressed, look under the clothes for any wear or moth damage (dresses and jumpers may conceal threadbare mohair or a replaced limb). Although a bear can usually be restored, certain damage, such as thin, rotting material, is extremely difficult to replace satisfactorily and should be avoided.

A History of Bear Collecting

Bears were first brought to public attention in the 19th century with the traveling dancing bears that performed in the streets before crowds of people. These provided the inspiration for the first bear-related items—wooden carved bears produced in Switzerland and Germany, known today as Black Forest bears. Other early bear products include pottery jugs made in Britain that depicted bears with rings through their noses, or bound in chains, inspired by the cruel sport of bear baiting.

The first soft toy bears appeared at the turn of the 20th century, standing on all fours and often mounted on wheels—Steiff in Germany and Martin and Pintel in France

A Black Forest wooden bear ornament

An early bear on wheels

both produced this type of bear. Postcards and books carried pictures and stories of bears, some of the grizzly variety, and many others based on traditional folk tales passed down over the years. One of the most famous is *Goldilocks and The Three Bears*, which was published in many languages.

But how did this bear of folk traditions turn into the childhood teddy we all know today?

There are numerous contenders for the first teddy bear, but perhaps the most famous and most documented claim is that made by the Americans. It is reported that when U.S. president Theodore Roosevelt went on a hunting trip to the Mississippi in 1902 he was unable to find a bear to kill. His supporters caught a bear cub and tied it to a tree for the president to shoot, but he refused to do it. This event was documented in the *Washington Post* on November 16, 1902, illustrated with the now-famous cartoon drawn by Clifford K. Berryman, entitled "Drawing the Line in Mississippi." The cartoon was an immediate

"Drawing the Line in Mississippi." Clifford Berryman's original version of the cartoon that appeared in the *Washington Post* on November 16, 1902

success and provoked a huge public response. Morris Michtom, a Russian emigré, was inspired by the events to produce his own toy bear to sell in his store in Brooklyn. He called it Teddy's Bear (Roosevelt's nickname was Teddy), allegedly having asked and been granted permission by Roosevelt himself to use the name. The rest is history. Michtom's entire stock of bears was purchased by U.S. whole-salers, Butler Brothers, who backed Michtom, enabling him set up what was allegedly the first teddy bear manufac-turer in the United States—the Ideal Novelty and Toy Co. By 1907 they were making bears on a large scale.

ABOVE The earliest "googly-eyed" bears produced by Ideal clearly resemble the bear in the Berryman cartoon

No. 11. The Roosevelt Bears at the Boston Public Library.
"They took the books and down they sat,
To read Emerson and the Autocrat."

LEFT Early postcards and books often depict realistic grizzly bears. Seymour Eaton's Teddy B and Teddy G, shown here, are typical

At the same time that bear fever was hitting the United States the teddy bear was gaining a foothold in Germany. Richard Steiff designed a plush bear for his aunt's toy factory in 1903, based on drawings that he had made of bears at the Stuttgart Zoo. Steiff's first bear—a Bar 55PB—attracted the attention of U.S. wholesaler George Borgfeldt when it was exhibited at the Leipzig Toy Fair, and he ordered 3,000. In 1905 Steiff registered the button-in-the-ear trademark, and in 1907 they called their bears "teddy." The word "teddy bear" did not appear in the dictionary until 1907, and it seems that most early bears were called "Bruin." It is alleged that U.S. author Seymour Eaton was the first person to use the word "teddy

Chiltern's first bear, a Master Teddy

other countries were also starting to make bears for the home market in the early years of the 20th century, including Britain, who found it easy to adapt their well-established toy-making skills to producing bears that are all very highly collectible today.

The start of the First World War in 1914 altered the face of bear manufacturing throughout the world, because bans on imported bears from Germany meant that countries were forced to make more bears for themselves—Chad Valley, Chiltern, and Farnell in Britain, Pintel and Fadap in France, and Joy Toys in Australia were all well-established as bear-makers by the 1920s. Early bears produced before the First World War tended to have boot-button eyes, but by the 1920s the eyes were gradually being replaced by glass. One exception was Britain, where manufacturers were requesting glass eyes for their bears as early as 1912. Early bears were hard-stuffed with excelsior, but after the First World War kapok, a softer and more cuddly alternative, was used.

LEFT An early Steiff from around 1905

RIGHT A lilac Farnell

bear" in one of his poems about the Roosevelt Bears, Teddy B and Teddy G, but it is generally agreed that the name was first used by Michtom.

There is also a British claim to having produced the first teddy bear, although possibly a more tenuous one. It is said that British King Edward VII fell in love with an Australian koala bear in London Zoo, and that in his honor the bear became known as Teddy Bear. The story may not be true, but it reflects the teddy bear fervor that existed at the time.

The years between 1906 and 1908 saw the height of the teddy bear craze, and were often referred to, particularly in the United States, as the "teddy bear years," coinciding as they did with President Roosevelt's second term in office (1905-9). Germany was the major manufacturer, producing many of its bears for export. But some

LEFT A blond Steiff from the 1920s

RIGHT A 1930s Yes/No Schuco bear with his original label

The 1920s saw the emergence of novelty bears, as manufacturers around the world competed for market dominance. Colored bears became very popular in the 1930s, with all the major manufacturers producing bears in vibrant shades of blue, red, green, and pink. The musical bears produced in Germany by Jopi are typical, made in bright colors and playing cheerful tunes. Bear clowns and jesters and dressed bears were also made at this time—Steiff was just one of the manufacturers to design a teddy clown. Novelty bears were produced all over the world, from Australia and Japan to Britain and Germany. German manufacturers Schuco and Gebruder Bing made bears that walked, danced, somersaulted, and even played ball. Miniatures were popular, the teddy bear powder compacts and perfume bottles of Schuco becoming adult fashion accessories. Winnie the Pooh and Rupert Bear also made their first appearances in print at this time.

By the 1930s new materials were being used, such as artificial silk plush, and a variation on the teddy bear —the panda bear—emerged after the panda's introduction to captivity in zoos in the United States and Britain—Merrythought, Chiltern and Gund all made soft toy pandas in the 1930s.

A synthetic plush panda produced by Gund in the 1940s

The Second World War in 1939 virtually put a stop to all toy manufacturing because all materials and labor had to be put toward munitions. Many factories had to close down and never reopened, and those that did make bears had to change their designs: bears made during the austerity of the Second World War were cut from more economical patterns and often have shorter limbs and smaller bodies. One solution was to dress bears, allowing the concealed body to be made from cotton, which was less expensive than mohair.

After the Second World War, many new manufacturers set up business in the U.S. zone of Germany, and the rest of the world also gradually started to recover from the restrictions imposed during the War. Bears were made from any fabrics that were available, often wool and cotton. The expensive kapok and wood wool stuffing that was used before the War was often replaced afterward by inexpensive cotton waste, know as sub-stuffing, which was made up of factory leftovers.

In 1948, British teddy bear manufacturer Wendy Boston patented the first lock-in safety eyes. Synthetic materials were patented and provided a less expensive alternative to mohair for bears. In 1960, it was Wendy Boston again who introduced the first washable teddy bear, made of nylon and stuffed with foam—her bears could even be put in the washing machine.

Two washable Wendy Boston bears

ABOVE One of the many bears that appeared on the market in the 1930s dressed as clowns

RIGHT A 1920s mechanical Schuco bear dressed in military uniform

The 1960s and 1970s saw a distinct move away from the traditional bears of the beginning of the century toward more mass-produced designs. Increasing competition from East Asia made it impossible for a number of the early manufacturers to continue trading —virtually all the factories in Australia had ceased business in the 1970s, as had those in France, and in Britain many manufacturers were bought out by larger companies who started to import toys from the Far East. However, those that did survive—Dean's in England, Steiff in Germany, Ideal in America to name but a few— continued to produce high-quality bears that managed to recapture the traditional feel of their early toys, and these are highly collectible today. It was also at this time that many teddy bear characters were being popularized by television programs, and soft toy versions of Paddington Bear, Winnie the Pooh, and Rupert were all made.

The first artist bears—modern hand-made exclusives— were produced on the west coast of the United States in the 1970s, and within a few years countries as far apart as New Zealand, Japan, Holland, Switzerland, and Austria followed suit. Today teddy bear artistry has become a highly important business, with as many people collecting artist bears as traditional examples, and whole fairs are often dedicated to artist bears alone.

LEFT Two bears produced by Applause in the 1980s with characteristic molded faces

RIGHT Artist bears by English artist, Jennie Sharman-Cox

In 1980 Steiff introduced the first-ever teddy bear replica, producing modern copies of a number of their traditional bears, in limited editions. Now replicas are made by most of the surviving long-established factories, including Merrythought and Dean's in Britain, Thiennot in France, and Steiff and Gebrüder Hermann in Germany. Many manufacturers, recognizing the collectibility of old bears, are now producing special limited and anniversary editions, aimed specifically at the collectors' market. Some, including Steiff and Dean's, even have their own collectors' clubs.

Such is the status of the teddy bear today that auction houses have sales specifically for teddy bears. Record-breaking prices have been reached in recent years and famous and celebrity bears are now often the subject of worldwide media coverage.

RIGHT Teddy Rose, originally made in 1925, was produced as a replica by Steiff in a limited edition of 10,000 in 1987

FAR RIGHT The House of Nisbet produced this replica of British television's *Brideshead Revisited* bear, Aloysius, in 1987—he even has replica patches on his pads and body

1865–1910

1865 Ignaz and Adolf Bing set up Gebrüder Bing in Germany

1886 Margarete Steiff starts making toys in Germany

1897 J.K. Farnell established as toy-makers in England by John Farnell

1902 Steiff produces its first bear, a Bär 55PB

1902 Clifford K. Berryman's famous cartoon appears in the *Washington Post* in the U.S.

1903 Dean's Rag Book Co. set up by Henry Samuel Dean in England

The first U.S. teddy bear manufacturer, the Ideal Toy & Novelty Co., is established

1905 Seymour Eaton's Roosevelt Bear stories published in the U.S.

1905 Steiff registers its button-in-the-ear trademark

1907 Bing makes its first bears

1907 Seymour Eaton uses the word "teddy bear" in his poem

1907 The Laughing Roosevelt bear introduced by the Columbia Teddy Bear Manufacturers in the U.S.

1907 *The Teddy Bear's Picnic* written by John Bratton in England

1908 Steiff introduces bears with tilt growlers

1908 The Chiltern Toy Works established by Joseph Eisenman

1911–1920

1911 Pintel et Fils in France produces its first bear, a mechanical tumbling clown

1912 Schreyer & Co. is founded by Henrich Müller and Henrich Schreyer in Germany

1912 Steiff introduces bears with glass eyes

1912 U.S. President Roosevelt fails to be reelected President

1914 The outbreak of the First World War and the ensuing ban on imported teddy bears from Germany leads to the establishment of toy manufacturers through the world

1915 Chad Valley produces its first teddy bears

1915 The Chiltern Toy Works produces its first bear, Master Teddy

1916 Harwin & Co. produces its Ally mascot bears in Britain for the First World War

1919 Emile Thiennot establishes his bear-making factory in France

1920 Max Hermann sets up Hermann Spielwaren in Germany

1920 Knickerbocker produces its first bears in the U.S.

1920 Mary Tourtel's Rupert Bear cartoon character makes his first appearance in the British *Daily Mail* newspaper

1920s Joy Toys starts making bears in Australia

1921–1930

1921 Schreyer & Co. officially registered as Schuco in Germany and produces its first Yes/No bear

1921 An Alpha Farnell bear is bought from Harrods in London for A.A. Milne's son, Christopher Robin, providing the inspiration for the Winnie the Pooh stories

1923 Chiltern introduces its Hugmee line of bears

1924 Chiltern Toys officially registered as a trademark

1924 A.A. Milne's first collection of verse, *When We Were Very Young*, published by Methuen in Britain.

c.1925 Gebrüder Süssenguth makes its Peter Bear in Germany

1925 J.K Farnell officially registers the Alpha trademark

1925 Fadap starts making bears

1928 Steiff introduces its Petsy bear, and dual-plush bears become popular with a number of other toy manufacturers

1929 Artificial silk plush used by British manufacturers, such as Farnell and Chiltern

1930s Bernhard Hermann establishes Gebrüder Hermann in Germany

1930 Merrythought registers its trademark in Britain

1930 First soft toy versions of Winnie the Pooh produced

1931–1950

1930s Novelty and colored bears become popular. Steiff introduces the Teddy Clown

1931 Merrythought introduces its Bingie range of dressed bears

1932 Bing ceases production

1935 J.K. Farnell opens a new factory after the previous one burns down

c.1935 Blinky Bill cartoon koala introduced to Australia

1937 A giant panda is introduced to Chicago Zoo, the first in the West, inspiring U.S. manufacturers to produce soft toy versions

1938 Chad Valley is appointed official toymaker to the Queen and starts printing this information on its labels

1938 Panda bears are introduced to London Zoo, inspiring a number of British manufacturers, including Merrythought and Chiltern, to make soft toy versions.

1938 Knickerbocker introduces shaved inset muzzles on its bears

1939 The outbreak of the Second World War leads to the closure of many soft toy manufacturers throughout the world

1945 The end of the Second World War leads to a great shortage of materials. Teddy bears develop shorter limbs and smaller bodies and start to appear in any available materials

1951–1970

1950s Synthetic materials become widely available and are adopted by toy manufacturers for their bears

1951 Steiff patents a new Original Teddy design

1951 Over 25 French manufacturers are listed at the French toy fair, the *Salon du Jouet*

1951 A shaggy dual-plush Zotty bear is introduced by Steiff, inspiring a number of other manufacturers to follow suit

1952 Chad Valley is granted the sole right to make the Sooty glove puppet based on British comedian Harry Corbet's television show

1953 The U.S. Forestry Commission employs the Ideal Novelty Company to produce its Smokey Bear fire prevention mascot

1953 The coronation of Queen Elizabeth II in Britain. Chad Valley's warrant transferred to the Queen Mother

1954 Wendy Boston in England produces the first washable bear

1957 Merrythought introduces its range of Cheeky bears

1958 Michael Bond's *A Bear Called Paddington* is published in Britain

1967 Chiltern is taken over by Chad Valley, producing bears with a Chad Valley/Chiltern label

1970 Schuco ceases business

1971 to present day

1970s The first artist bears are conceived on the West Coast of the U.S.

1971 Joy Toys ceases production

1972 British designer Gabrielle Clarkson creates the first soft toy version of Paddington Bear

1975 Eden Toys gains world rights for the soft toy production of Paddington Bear

1976 Pintel ceases trading

1978 Fadap ceases trading

1978 The North American Bear Company is set up in America

1979 The North American Bear Company's Very Important Bear series is launched

1980 Steiff introduces replicas

1982 The Applause division of Knickerbocker is bought by Harris Toibb of Wallace Berrie

1985 Sotheby's of London holds its first sale devoted to teddy bears

1988 The British chainstore Woolworths takes over the Chad Valley name when Chad ceases business

1989 "Happy," a Steiff from c.1926, sells for the record-breaking price of £55,000 ($80,000) at Sotheby's in London

1994 Teddy Girl sells at Christie's for a record-breaking price of £110,000 ($176,000)

Bears of the World

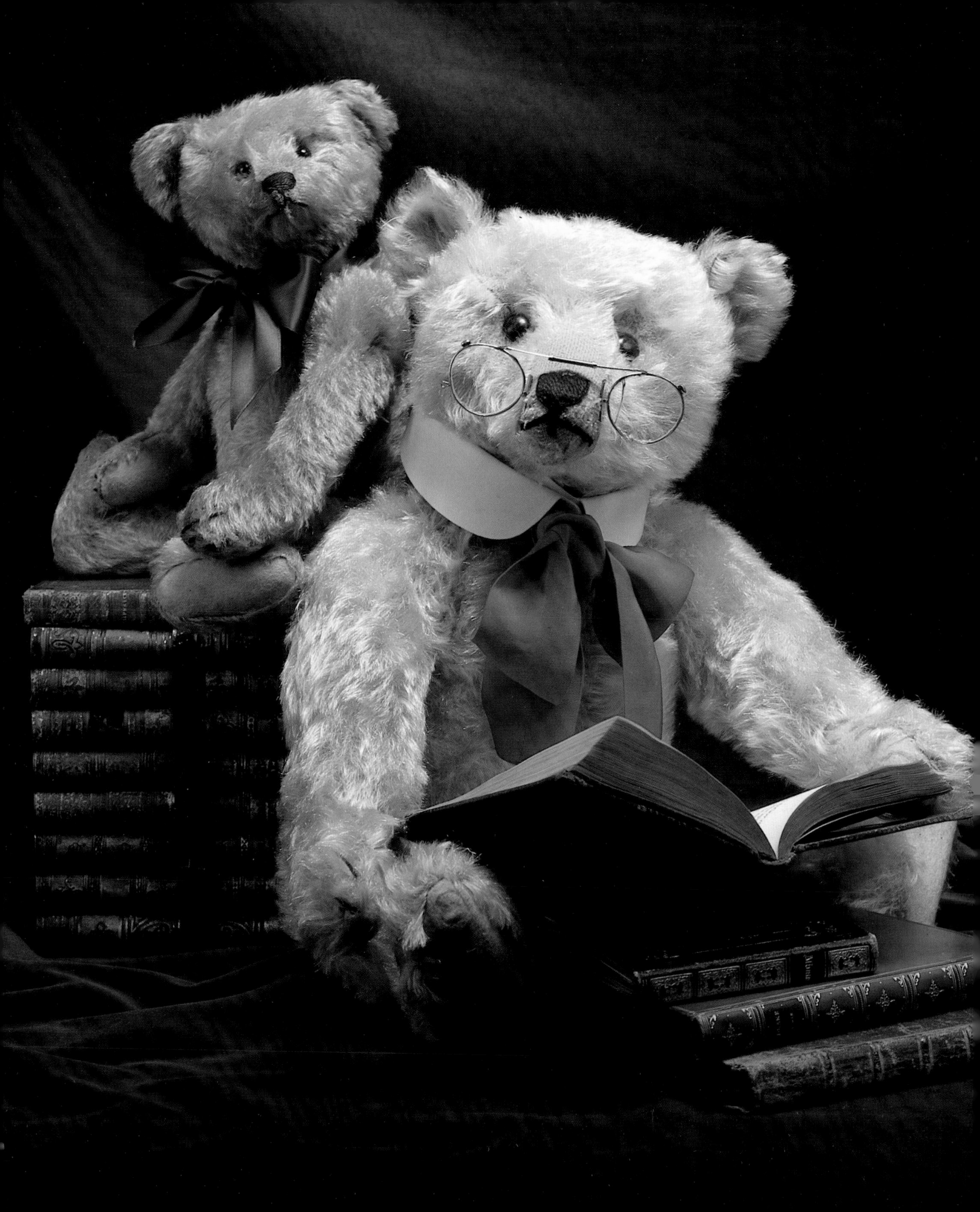

German Bears

Germany has a long tradition of toymaking, and the Sonneberg Neustadt area is famous throughout the world for its production of dolls and toys. Two notable manufacturers producing bears outside this region are the Steiff factory, about two hundred miles (320km) south of Sonneberg, and Bing in Nuremberg. As well as housing some of the major German manufacturers, the Sonneberg region was also home to hundreds of cottage industries where whole families, including the children, made a vast number of bears, usually in cramped conditions in one room. They worked to fill the huge demand for bears from the rest of the world. Many of the bears were unmarked, and few of them can be traced to a manufacturer today. Among the names that stand out in the German bear-making world are Steiff, Schuco, Bing, Gebrüder Sussenguth, and Hermann, but a number of lesser-known manufacturers also produced bears that are popular with collectors, including Eduard Crämer. German bears are famous for their very high quality, and there is great demand for them throughout the world.

LEFT Two early Steiffs, one a rare cinnamon color, enjoying some books together.

RIGHT An early rod-jointed Steiff bear from around 1904 with an elephant button in his ear.

Steiff

The internationally famous firm of Steiff was started in 1877 in Germany by Margarete Steiff, who, crippled with polio and confined to a wheelchair, made stuffed toys using felt left over from her uncle's fabric factory. When her nephew, Richard, joined the firm he introduced bears based on sketches he had drawn during his visits to the Stuttgart Zoo. The very first bear, made in 1902, was a 55 PB with very primitive joints attached by a string. It was presented at the Spring Fair in Leipzig in 1903, and although the initial reception was poor, a buyer from the major New York importer, George Borgfeldt and Co., placed a sizable order. There are no recorded details of these earliest bears, and none are known to have survived. Richard continued to work on the design, and the result was a smaller, less plump bear with improved joints and light mohair plush, registered in 1904 as Bär 35 PB. It was received with great acclaim, and by the end of the year, 12,000 had been sold. In 1904, the 28 PB, a smaller version of the 35 PB, was offered, with newly patented metal-rod joints, and in 1905 the highly successful 35 PAB was introduced. Steiffs are probably the most sought-after bears, perhaps because the tilt of their heads and expressive faces make them irrestistible to collectors worldwide.

RIGHT Although Steiff's 35 PB had simple thread jointing, the 28 PB had a firm metal rod passed through its body (giving it the name Rod bear). These two PBs were the only designs offered by Steiff between 1904 and 1905, and are the earliest of their bears to have survived. They are very different from later Steiffs, with realistically long arms and curved paws, which enabled them to stand on all fours.
Height: *white bear* 16in (40cm); *beige bear* 18in (45cm)
Approx value: $9,000–15,000 each

LEFT The PB Rod bear takes its name from the metal rods which are passed through the body to hold it together, visible in the x-ray in this picture. The rods, together with the tightly packed wood wool and kapok stuffing, made Rod bears much less cuddly than later examples, and consequently they were not very popular with children. Many have a seam running across the top of the head where they were left open for stuffing. Early bears had five claws on their paws and feet.
Height: 20in (40cm)
Approx value: $12,000–15,000

ABOVE The PAB is one of the first bears to be made with cardboard joints. He is softer than the Rod bear and is very light because he is stuffed with kapok and excelsior.
Height: 28in (71cm)
Approx value: $7,500–9,000

LEFT The rare muzzled bear in this picture is extremely prized. It is based on the performing bears that toured the circuses in Europe and the United States. The fact that these bears, both from around 1910, are in excellent condition makes them very desirable.
Height: *left* 15¹/₂in (40cm); *right* 13in (33cm)
Approx value: $6,000–9,000

Cone-shaped
nose, 1904–5

Center-seam nose

ABOVE In the early years every seventh bear made by Steiff had a seam down the center of his head, to enable the firm to make the most economical use of the fabric. This seam gives the bears the appealing expression seen on this example from around 1907, and makes them much sought-after by collectors. Originally, the seam would not have been so visible through the thick plush, but on worn examples it is quite clear.
Height: 16in (40.5cm)
Approx value: $5,700–6,800

ABOVE The facial expression greatly affects the price of a Steiff bear; this cinnamon Steiff has a particularly appealing face. The remains of a white label and his tilt growler date him to after 1908, when these features were introduced by Steiff.
Height 25in (63.5cm)
Approx value: $6,000–9,000

Sealing wax
nose, 1904–5

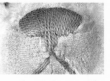

Typical nose,
1905

Light stitching used
on white bears

Nose used on bears
under 16 inches
(40.6cm)

RIGHT Two of the most desirable and rare colors of mohair for Steiff bears are cinnamon and white. "Montgomery," made around 1907, has the typical light-brown stitching used by Steiff on their white mohair bears. His large flat feet have cardboard inserts, a feature on many larger bears. Sometimes, on early Steiff bears, the top layer of felt on the paw pads has peeled away to reveal a different color felt underneath. These might be different on both feet, either red, blue, or green depending on the cloth available when the bear was being made; on later bears these colors were replaced by

neutral shades. This bear has the typically long arms of Steiff's early bears. Another Steiff characteristic is the hand-sewn seam down the stomach.
Height: 25in (63.5cm)
Approx value: $6,000–9,000

Profile of a Rod bear, 1904-5, showing the typically long muzzle, long limbs, upturned paws, and pronounced hump on his back.

1905 cone-nosed bear has a much rounder muzzle. Paws are large and spoon-shaped with five black-stitched claws.

By c.1907 the Steiff body has become chunkier, and the muzzle is more defined. Limbs are still long.

In the 1920s Steiff bears still had long arms and large feet, but the body had become a little plumper than earlier.

The 1951 Original Teddy has distinctly shorter limbs, a rounder face, and fatter body than earlier designs.

LEFT The perfect condition of this delightful rare-colored cinnamon bear from 1910 suggests rather sadly that he was never played with, which is hard to understand as his quirky nose stitching gives him a very appealing face.

Cinnamon bears in good condition are rare because the color fades quickly if exposed to too much light. The fur on these bears can be sparse, as the dye seems to weaken the material.
Height: 16in (40.5cm)
Approx value: $6,000-9,000

LEFT It is typical of small Steiff bears like the one on the left of this picture to have no felt paw pads. He was made around 1912 and has glass eyes, which were introduced at this time to satisfy the demand of the British market. Soon they replaced boot-button eyes altogether. The bear's larger companion dates from around 1920. Both have gold bristle mohair, which was popular for smaller bears and miniatures.
Height: *left* 5in (11cm); *right* 9in (23cm)
Approx value: *left* $600-750; *right* $750-900

LEFT This black bear does not have the usual red felt around the eyes, and this makes him particularly rare. He is in excellent condition and has luxuriant long mohair. His black button eyes and long, jointed limbs are typical of early Steiffs. He is the same style as the bear on the right, but looks fatter because his mohair is in better condition.
Height: 20in (41cm)
Approx value: $27,000-30,000

RIGHT Steiff made this black bear as part of a special order for the British market in 1912. Unlike the eyes of the bear on the left, which are difficult to see, the eyes on this bear have the traditional red felt around them to give them greater definition. Often the mohair coat on black bears appears faded and worn, but this example has kept its color and is still in good condition, which will add to its collectibility.
Height: 15in (38cm)
Approx value: $12,000-15,000

Elephant button, 1904-5

Blank button, 1905-9

1905-50 Steiff with underscored "f"

BUTTONS

The Button-in-the-Ear trademark was patented by Steiff in 1905 to stop other manufacturers from copying their designs. The first Steiff label was a cardboard tag printed with an elephant with an "S"-shaped trunk. These were easily lost, so Steiff introduced a more permanent means of identification, a metal button attached to the left ear with two prongs. The early buttons were embossed with an elephant logo, but in 1905 this was changed for the word "Steiff." Between 1904 and 1905 a blank button was sometimes used. Cloth labels were attached to the buttons in 1908. Buttons and labels changed many times, and old stocks were used at the same time as new ones. Paper tags have always been used with the metal buttons (see p.30).

1920-50 slightly larger button

1920-50s button

Late 1930s brass button

Blank button, 1948-50

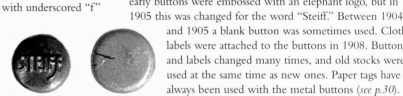

1950-2

1952-70

1952-70 used for woolen miniatures

1965 chrome button

1979 brass button

Blank brass button used on seconds from 1984

ABOVE These two bears have been life-long companions ever since they were made around 1920. When they appeared for sale at a London auction house in 1994, they were accompanied by a plea that they should stay together. The larger standing bear is actually a rare teddy bear rattle which when shaken still emits a noise. Although the mohair looks gray now it was originally white. He has brown and black glass eyes, and as with many small bears, has no felt paw pads. His tiny companion has short clipped golden bristle mohair. His knitted sweater is unlikely to be original.
Height: *back* 5in (13cm); *front* 3½in (9cm)
Approx value: $600–900 each

LEFT This Bär Dolly (Dolly-Bear) is particularly sought-after by collectors because he is not only very rare, but is also one of a limited number of bears produced to commemorate a historically important event. Made in the United States' national colors of red, white, and blue, these bears were specially produced for the 1912 Presidential election in which Theodore Roosevelt failed to be reelected to office. The bears came in three sizes, 10, 12, and 13 inches (20.5, 30.5, and 33cm), and were produced between 1912 and 1916.
This particular example is in excellent condition. He has a red mohair body and limbs, white mohair face, white wool neck ruff, and black boot-button eyes. Although a novelty bear, he still has the distinctive Steiff hump on his back and metal button in his ear.
Height: 12in (30cm)
Approx value: $15,000–18,000

LEFT By the 1920s the profile of the head had become slightly flatter, although the arms were still characteristically long. At this time Steiff started to make more frequent use of kapok (previously mixed with excelsior), which made the bear lighter and softer.
Height: 24in (61cm)
Approx value: $3,800–5,300

BELOW These charming dancing bears from around 1920 are locked together in close embrace by stitching! The couple is particularly rare because they still have their original clothes, which are in excellent condition. The bears are typical of those made by Steiff in the 1920s, with the horizontal nose stitching of smaller bears, and brown and black glass eyes. The Steiff embossed button is clearly visible on the male bear's left ear. Dressed Steiff bears are rare and sought-after by collectors, and the fact that this particular couple is the only one known will add to its value considerably.
Height: *male dancer* 12in (30cm); *female dancer* 11½in (28cm)
Approx value: $12,000–15,000

STEIFF ANIMALS

The first soft toy made by Margarete Steiff was an elephant, designed as a pin cushion but soon adopted by children who until this time were used to playing with uncuddly wooden toys. Animals other than teddy bears have featured widely in Steiff's catalogs ever since: their catalog for 1911/12 has 1,700 different species. Dogs and cats were the most popular animals in the mid-1920s, made of plush rather than the felt of earlier examples. Generally, smaller animals were made in greater quantities than the larger ones and are more readily available today. There is now a growing trend for collecting Steiff animals, not only to complement bear collections, but also to build up a collection of a particular type of animal (i.e. dog, cat, or rabbit), or a whole menagerie.

Steiff's attempts to capture the character of the popular British comic strip pup, Bonzo, were not liked by the pup's creator George Studdy, and only 115 were made. This example, from around 1920, is musical, and is worked by a bellows movement in his chest.
Height: 17in (43cm)
Approx value: $3,000-4,500

Peter Rabbit was made up until the First World War, but this one can be dated to around 1905 by the elephant stamp on the sole of his left slipper, and his button eyes. The rabbits were made only for the British market.
Height: 12in (30.5cm)
Approx value: $1,200-1,800

From their early days Steiff produced soft toy cats. This example dates from around 1935. When the tail is moved around, the head turns in a circle.
Height: 10in (25cm)
Approx value: $450-600

Steiff made only 1,400 of these wonderful Puss in Boots cats in three sizes, between 1912 and 1917. This fine example has managed to keep all his original clothing, even down to the wooden sword and feather in his cap.
Height: 17in (43cm)
Approx value: $4,500-6,000

"Pummy Rabbit" is one of Steiff's later animal designs, produced in 1963. He displays the typical high quality of their animals and still has his original paper chest tag and Steiff button in his ear.
Height: 10in (25cm)
Approx value: $75-90

"Caesar," made by Steiff in 1910, was modeled on the favorite dog of King Edward VII. He has a leather disk around his neck with his name on it.
Height: 10in (25cm)
Approx value: $400-600

"Peky" is typical of the animals Steiff produced in the 1960s. Although inexpensive at the moment, the value of this dog will appreciate in the future.
Height: 10in (25cm)
Approx value: $75-90

LABELS AND TAGS
Below is a selection of some of the different types of labels and tags used by Steiff alongside the metal buttons (*see p.26*). They should be regarded only as a general reference, as like the metal buttons, designs have changed many times during the factory's history, and not all of them can be shown here.

Early elephant stamp on foot, 1904-5

1926-8 chest label

1928-50 chest label

1990s material label

ABOVE Steiff's Gallop bears are so-named because they perform amusing galloping movements when they are pulled along in their riding frame. They were part of Steiff's novelty range that they introduced in the 1920s to meet competition from rival companies.
Height: 4in (10cm)
Approx value: $2,300-3,000

ABOVE Steiff introduced its series of Roly Droly animals in the mid-1920s. When pulled along, the two animals on the vehicle move in opposite directions. Other examples bore different animals.
Height: 6in (15cm)
Approx value: $3,000-4,500

RIGHT In the 1920s Steiff introduced new colors to their range of mohair plush bears. This very rare example, in brown and cream dual plush (tipped mohair), is similar to the Petsy bears on the next page. Dual plushes in other colors were also made; the tipped effect is created by lightly brushing the surface of the mohair with a darker dye. Distinctive features of this bear are his particularly large black and brown painted glass eyes and his large ears set wide apart on the side of his head. He is stuffed with kapok. This bear has an embossed metal button but he also has traces of a red material label. This helps to date the bear, because the red label was used by Steiff only between 1925 and 1935.
Height: 17in (43cm)
Approx value: $9,000-12,000

RIGHT The Record line of bears was produced by Steiff between 1913 and the 1950s. The line consisted of bears and other animals which, when pulled along on a 4-wheeled chassis, made a back-and-forth rowing movement. A pair of bellows was fixed to the rear axle to produce a noise.
Height: 10in (25cm)
Approx value: $11,300–15,000

LEFT The Record Petsy shown here is very rare and highly sought-after; only 1,462 examples were produced, for just one year, between 1928 and 1929. The bear has all the typical Petsy features, including dual mohair plush and blue googly eyes (see the Petsy bear pictured below).
Height: 10in (25cm)
Approx value: $6,800–7,500

LEFT Despite their similarity in looks, only the small bear in this picture is actually a Petsy bear. Petsy bears were introduced in 1928, and were produced for only a very short time. They are very rare and highly prized today. The bears were soft-filled and had white mohair tipped with reddish brown. One of the most distinctive features of Petsy bears is the seam that runs down the front and back of the head and across to the ears. Other typical features include a pink nose, blue googly eyes (based on the big eyes in 1920s cartoons), and a voice box, which was either automatic, or operated by a squeeze box. The ears were wired so that they could be moved to give the bear an endearing expression. Although the bear on the right of the picture has blue eyes, they are not googly. Also, rather than the pink nose, he has light gold stitching. The bear on the left is lighter in color, but has dark nose stitching, which is an unusual feature on Steiff's dual-colored bears.
Height: *left* 24in (60cm); *right* 20in (50cm); *front* 12in (30cm)
Approx value: $4,500–11,300 each

BELOW Steiff added a number of novelty bears to its range in the 1920s to meet changing tastes at home and abroad. The Teddy Clown is a typical example, designed to capture the mood of the 1920s. Only 30,000 of these clowns were produced by Steiff, between 1926 and 1928, in 11 different sizes, ranging from 9 to 45 inches (23 to 114cm). They were all fitted with a two-colored hat and ruff of blue and white, or red and white, but these are often missing. To see a group of five clowns in such perfect condition as these is unusual. The bear on the left is particularly rare because he still has his original paper label. These bears have tipped mohair, but others were made in pink or gold.
Height: 6in (15cm) to 19in (48cm)
Approx value: $4,500–9,000 each

RIGHT Teddy Baby, modeled on a bear cub, was developed by Steiff as a humorous character. The first were made in 1930, but the design remained popular with children right up until the late 1950s. Some were made with closed mouths, but these are rare today. The most collectible Teddy Baby is white.
Height: 18in (46cm)
Approx value: $1,200–1,800

LEFT Steiff's miniature bears have no paw stitching or felt pads. These bears date from 1920 to 1950 (left to right). The earlier bears are skinnier with further-apart ears and more pointed faces.
Height: 3 to 3$\frac{1}{2}$in (7.5 to 9cm)
Approx value: $375 to $750 each

BELOW In 1951 Steiff created a new pattern for its Original Teddy, which is significantly different from the designs of their earlier bears. The arms are now shorter and straighter, and the body is a little plumper. The face is also much rounder, with a muzzle which is not at all pronounced, and ears that are closer together. The nose is no longer stitched horizontally, but vertically. Original Teddy was produced in a variety of different colors, but the white plush of the example shown here was the most common.
Height: 26in (66cm)
Approx value: $3,000-3,750

ABOVE Only 897 examples of this Circus Bear were made (from 1935 to 1939). When his tail is twisted his head moves in a circular direction.
Height: 13in (33cm)
Approx value: $4,500-6,000

ABOVE Modern Steiff bears are quite different from earlier examples, with straight limbs and shaving around the muzzle and between the eyes.
Height: 30in (76cm)
Approx value: $375-750

Top five best-selling Steiff bears at auction

1 "Teddy Girl," December 1994, Christie's, London, $176,000 (£110,000)

2 "Happy," September 1989, Sotheby's, London, $88,000 (£55,000)

3 "Eliot," December 1993, blue Steiff, Christie's, London, $79,200 (£49,500)

4 "Othello," May 1990, 1912 black, center-seam Steiff, Sotheby's, London, $38,700 (£24,200)

5 Rare black Steiff, December 1994, Christie's, London, $35,200 (£22,000)

Bing

Ignaz and Adolf Bing founded Gebrüder Bing in Nüremberg in 1865 to produce tin and kitchenware, and in around 1890 they started making enameled and tin toys. In 1907, when the teddy bear boom was at its height, they made their first bears. Initially these had a metal arrow in their ear, with the initials G.B.N. set in a diamond, but this is usually missing today. Steiff immediately started litigation against Bing for using the tag in the ear, beause it was so close to their own methods of identification, so Bing put a metal button underneath the arm instead. However, Steiff still objected to the word "button," so Bing had to remove it from their catalog and replace it with "G.B.N. label under the arm." Eventually, Bing stopped using the tag altogether, replacing it around 1920 with a metal label attached to the right arm.

Bing is particularly famous for its mechanical bears, introduced around 1910, but these are very rare today. Although early Bings are similar in style to Steiffs, after 1920 Bing changed its design: the later bears have a longer snout with distinctive stitching on the muzzle, and a very wide smile. Bing stopped producing bears in 1932, and consequently Bing bears are far more difficult to find than those made by Steiff, especially outside of Germany. Bings have very appealing faces and are greatly sought after by collectors throughout the world. The condition of those featured on these pages is exceptional.

RIGHT Bing's mechanical bears share the same features as their non-mechanical counterparts: apart from its mechanism this bear from 1908 is very similar to the non-mechanical one in the inset picture. Particularly notable are the wide head with small ears set at the corners, the long arms and body, and large oval feet (very different from the narrow feet of Steiff bears). When the key is wound the bear moves his head from side to side. The mechanism is durable, but if it breaks it is very hard to repair. This bear has his original claw stitching, but replacement felt paw pads.
Height: 15in (38cm)
Approx value: $3,000

RIGHT By 1915 the face of Bing bears had changed slightly from that of the earlier design. The features are very small in relation to the head, giving the bears the endearing expression that so many collectors adore, and the muzzle is slightly more pointed. This bear has a long white silky mohair coat and light-colored nose and claw stitching. Bings of 16 inches (40cm) and under have nose stitching almost identical to the horizontal stitching of the Steiff nose, and sometimes the bears from these two makers can be confused.
Height: 13in (33cm)
Approx value: $2,700

ABOVE By the 1920s the muzzle became significantly longer and was shaved, and the eyes were closer together The rare white color and exceptional quality of the mohair of this bear make him particularly desirable.
Height: 20in (51cm)
Approx value: $6,000

LEFT The worn pad on this bear's left foot reveals that he does not have the cardboard inserts used on Bing's larger bears up until 1920, the time this bear was probably made. He has the typically wide shaved muzzle and large head of later Bings, although his short mohair is quite rare.
Height: 24in (61cm)
Approx value: $2,300-3,000

LEFT This wonderful bear displays all the typical characteristics of Bings made in the late 1920s, including long silky mohair, large head and ears, long pronounced shaved muzzle, curved paws, and short arms. One of the most notable changes from the design of early Bings is the large smiling mouth, which now extends the width of the muzzle.
Height: 17in (43cm)
Approx value: $6,800

ABOVE Small non-mechanical Bing bears from the 1920s are very rare, and this example is even more unusual because it has the short bristle mohair usually associated with their mechanical bears. Like small Steiffs, this bear has no paw pads. The long shaved snout is typical of Bing's bears from this time. His B.W. label is clearly visible on his right arm.
Height: 8in (20cm)
Approx value: $1,800

LEFT It is unusual to find such a large Bing as the one shown here, which stands 31 inches (79cm) high. Despite his size he displays all the typical characteristics of smaller Bings, including large ears and pointed feet. Because it can be difficult to display such a large bear, the use of a child's sleigh here is a perfect solution. Other suitable props for large bears include children's chairs and high chairs (*see p.171*).
Height: 31in (79cm)
Value: $9,000

LEFT This rare hanging bear was the subject of a lawsuit in 1910 by Steiff, who claimed it was copied from their very similar Purzel-Bär, made in 1909. The bears have hooks on the ends of the paw pads that extend from metal rods in the arms. The clock-work mechanism is activated by winding the arms back, causing the bear to somersault. Despite the rather fragile and worn condition of this example, he still works.
Height: 13in (33cm)
Approx value: $1,500

LEFT Dark brown Bings are rarely seen, and one with such a beautiful coat as this example will be particularly prized. A number of Bings from this time have the bright orange and black glass eyes seen on this bear, and these may be helpful when trying to identify bears that have lost their labels. The cream paw pads are in very strong contrast to the color of the rest of the bear.
Height: 19in (48cm)
Approx value: $6,800

Engraved label from c.1910

Metal label, c.1919, used on right arm

Penguin's label, c.1918

Metal label, used on right arm until 1930

ABOVE Similarities between this tipped Bing bear and those made by Steiff (*see p.30*) are obvious. But the Bing can be identified by his long claws and his nose. Although the same shape as a Steiff nose, the Bing stitching is slightly different.
Height: 17in (44cm)
Approx value: $4,500-5,500

ABOVE The white of this long mohair is another very rare color for Bings, and this, together with its perfect condition, make the bear particularly collectible. Typical of paler-colored bears, he has light-brown nose and claw stitching.
Height: 14in (35.5cm)
Approx value: $4,500

RIGHT Bing also produced a number of mechanical bears in white mohair. This example from around 1910 has the light nose stitching featured on the paler bears, although in this case the color is particularly bright. This bear has a key-wind mechanism, which when activated moves the bear's head from side to side.
Height: 21in (53cm)
Approx value: $6,800

LEFT Bing animals were made in both mohair and felt. This delightful penguin from 1915 has a mohair body and felt feet, beak and inside flippers. The metal disk attached to the left flipper has the initials G.B.N., set in a triangle. On the other side is written "I am your luck (*sic*) Penguin/from distant rocky shore/behave myself quite genuine/and when you squeeze me snore."
Height: 14in (35.5cm)
Approx value: $680

LEFT Not many of Bing's mechanical bears have survived, but the type most likely to to be found is a roller skater like this one. He is attached to metal skates and has a walking stick fixed to his right arm, which moves up and down causing the bear to tilt backwards and forwards as he skates along. Like fellow German manufacturer, Schuco, Bing used short bristle mohair for its mechanical small bears. A distinctive characteristic of these bears is the left arm held straight out in front of the body.
Height: 8in (20cm)
Approx value: $4,500-5,300

LEFT This bear on skis is almost identical to the roller skater. The metal label on his right arm has "B.W." printed on it, and is of a type used from around 1919. These bears have also been found without the label, and it is believed that they were made earlier (perhaps from 1912 on). It is very unusual to find Bing mechanical bears still with their clothes on, particularly when they are in such perfect condition as the four seen here. This bear even has his original paper price tag up his sleeve—for $1.69!
Height: 8in (20cm)
Approx value: $4,500-5,300

From c.1907	c.1916–1920s	1920–30
Round head	Wide head	Very large head
Small ears set on the side of the head	Slightly larger ears set on side of head	Very large ears set on top of head
Boot-button eyes	Glass eyes	Orange glass eyes
Long arms, curved paws	Long arms, curved paws	Shorter arms, curved paws
High quality mohair	Quality mohair	Very long silky mohair
Vertical stitching on bears of 16 inches (40cm) and over, horizontal stitching on smaller bears	Vertical nose stitching on bears of 16 inches (40cm) and over, horizontal on smaller bears	Distinctive nose stitching on bears of 16 inches (40cm) and over, with a double stitch that runs under the middle stitches and frames the nose
Short unshaven muzzle	Muzzle becoming longer	Very long shaved muzzle
Small facial features		Very long smile extending the width of the muzzle
G.B.N. engraved metal button under the arm until c.1910	Metal tag under the arm, metal label on the body or a limb	Orange metal button with B.W. painted in black attached to right arm

LEFT This mechanical bear simply walks, and the photograph shows how the felt pads have worn because of his over-zealous traveling! He still wears his original felt clothes, which are in excellent condition. It is surprising that most of these bears have not lost their keys, considering their age. **Height:** 8in (20cm) **Approx value:** $4,500–5,300

BELOW Bing's tumbling bears are particularly sought after by collectors. This example is made of short brown mohair and is dressed in a felt shirt and jacket, and cotton pants. He has very long arms to enable him to tumble. Unlike the other mechanical bears shown here, this bear is not activated by a key; instead the arms are turned in a circular motion to set the tumbling mechanism in action. Also different from the others is his lack of paw pads. **Height:** 8in (20cm) **Approx value:** $4,500–5,300

Hermann-Spielwaren

Hermann-Spielwaren is one of the oldest family-owned teddy bear manufacturers in Germany, and together with Gebruder Hermann (*see pp. 42-3*) they form part of what is known today as the Hermann Teddy Bear Dynasty. The firm was founded in 1920 by Max Hermann under his own name, in a small village called Neufang, close to Sonneberg, the then toy capital of the world. He had already made bears with his brother Arthur and sister Adelheid in 1913, under the trade name of the Johann Hermann Toy Factory. Max Hermann moved his company to Sonneberg in 1923 and established himself as a world-wide name in bear manufacturing. At the beginning of the 1930s he designed his now-famous logo of a green triangle and a bear with a running dog, which is still in use today. Following the Second World War, Max and his family fled across the border to West Germany to escape the communist regime, and reestablished the business in Coburg, Bavaria, where it is still making bears to this day. For a short period between 1949 and 1953 Hermann bears were made at both Sonneberg and Coburg.

RIGHT This bear, made in Sonneberg in 1924, is the earliest-known Hermann bear. Typical features of this period are the glass eyes, the shaved mohair on the nose, the short muzzle, and the small feet, which were designed to save on expensive mohair fabric after the First World War. The bear is stuffed with excelsior and has replacement paw pads—the originals would have been felt. Replicas of this particular design have been produced by Hermann in recent years.
Height: 12in (30cm)
Approx value: $680

LEFT The fact that the chest tag on this light-brown mohair bear does not have the word "Hermann" on the back dates it to the early 1950s when the word was introduced. This bear has amber and black glass eyes and a shaved muzzle. The horizontal stitching on his nose and the three stitches on his paws are common characteristics of Hermann bears. Post-Second World War examples such as this have noticeably shorter limbs than those made before the War.
Height: 12in (30cm)
Approx value: $680

Earliest label, used until the 1940s

Late 40s-early 50s

Early-mid-50s

Mid-50s-early 60s

Early 60s-late 60s

Early 60s-70s, for dralon plush bears

Late 60s to present day

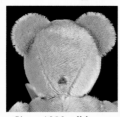

Since 1993, all bears have an identifying neckmark

LEFT Max Herrman made these three bears for a big toy exhibition staged in Germany in 1933 to celebrate the end of Black Friday. They are in perfect condition. They remained hidden in vaults in the Sonneberg Toy Museum until Max Hermann's son, Rolf, haunted by the memory of these bears, traveled to East Germany and found them in a chest in a corner of the musuem's archives. They are extremely rare.
Height: 7in (18cm) each
Approx value: $1,500 the set

ABOVE Unlike most of Hermann's tipped mohair bears, this example does not have the same fur on the in-side of his ears as on his body: instead he has hair to match his nose. He has the typically long muzzle (3$\frac{1}{2}$in, 9cm) of Hermann's larger bears. Made around 1950 in Sonneberg, he still has his original felt paws with three black embroi-dered stitches, and has a growler voice box. This particular bear was used by Hermann as a basis for their Old Max Replica Bear.
Height: 31$\frac{1}{2}$in (80cm)
Approx value: $530

ABOVE Hermann was one of the first manufacturers to machine sew the ears on their bears (introducing the process in the 1950s), and Hermann bears from this time onwards are much less likely to have lost their ears than earlier examples that had their ears sewn on by hand. Hermann bears tend to have the particularly small glass eyes seen on this example, made in 1955 in Coburg. He needs some attention to his paw pads as the felt has worn through, but this will not detract much from the value.
Height: 27$\frac{1}{2}$in (70cm)
Approx value: $600

ABOVE Hermann continues to produce bears today. This special edition bear was made in 1993 to commemorate the eightieth anniversary of the opening of Max Hermann's factory in 1913. As a tribute, the bear was made in a limited edition of 1,913. Made of mohair and stuffed with excelsior, the bear will be highly collectible in the future. By comparing this bear with the others in this section, it can be seen how Hermann's design has changed very little over the years.
Height: 17in (43cm)
Approx value: $600

Gebrüder Hermann

Bernhard Hermann began making teddy bears in Sonneberg in the 1930s, supplying the home market and a number of manufacturers in the United States. His four sons, Horst (who died in 1937), Hellmut, Artur, and Werner helped their father in his factory. In 1948 Bernhard relocated the business to Hirschaid, near Bambert in the U.S. zone of Germany, and in 1952 changed its name from Bernhard Hermann to the Hermann Brothers Company. Bernhard died in 1959, and the business was left to his sons. Gebrüder Hermann still produces very high quality bears by traditional methods, including using a funnel to hand-stuff the bears with excelsior. Noses are hand-stitched and only the finest materials are used. The early bears tend to have short mohair, and most have a shaved muzzle. Following the Second World War, the firm introduced its popular range of Zotty-type bears to rival those made by Steiff.

LEFT This 1930s bear displays many of the characteristics of Gebrüder Hermann's early bears. Perhaps most notable is his inset muzzle of clipped, golden mohair plush. Also typical are his large round head, round ears, and slim limbs. This example is in very good condition, although there is some variation in the color of his mohair. His sad face is particularly appealing.
Height: 29in (74cm)
Approx value: $825

CHARACTERISTICS OF EARLY HERMANN BEARS

• large round ears set on the sides of the head

• pronounced, clipped plush muzzle set into the face, often in a paler shade than the body

• black horizontally-stitched nose

• inverted "y"-shaped mouth

• upturned paws

• three black claw stitches

• slender limbs

LEFT Bernhard Hermann made his early bears in several different colors. This example was originally blue, but has faded to silver and is almost threadbare—his skin is showing through underneath! An identical bear was made in pink. Damage to the felt pads reveals his wood wool stuffing.
Height: 23in (58.5cm)
Approx value: $250

1929

1930–39

1945–51

since 1952

ZOTTY BEARS

Zotty bears were introduced by Steiff in 1951. They take their name from "*zottig*," the German word for shaggy. The bears are characterized by their long shaggy mohair and open felt mouths. They were very popular, and soon other German manufacturers copied the design. The bears are all very similar and if they are not labeled it can be difficult to tell who made them. A distinct difference between Steiff and Hermann Zotty bears is that the Steiff Zotties have a white bib whereas the Hermann bears do not.

BELOW This open-mouthed bear is in rather poor condition. Typical Hermann characteristics include the inset shaved muzzle, large cupped ears and upturned paws.
Height: 21in (43cm)
Approx value: $300

ABOVE LEFT Gebrüder Hermann was one of the many German manufacturers that made bears with open felt mouths based on the Steiff Zotty. This example, made by Hermann in the 1950s, is quite different from the Steiff Zotty because he is made from dark wool plush rather than the usual long shaggy tipped mohair. Comparisons with the bear on the right suggest that he has lost his mouth stitching.
Height: 14in (35.5cm)
Approx value: $375

ABOVE This Hermann Zotty-type bear is in excellent condition. He has the lovely cream-tipped mohair coat characteristic of these bears, and perfect felt paw pads. He also has his original card and red plastic swing tags, which make him easy to identify. However, even without this labeling, his downturned nose stitching and lack of white bib on his chest make it possible to identify him as a Hermann bear, rather than a Steiff.
Height: 15in (38cm)
Approx value: $400

Schuco

The firm of Schreyer and Co. was founded in Nuremberg in 1912 by Heinrich Schreyer, a furniture salesman, and Heinrich Müller, who had previously worked at Gebrüder Bing (*see pp.34-9*). Initially they produced mechanical tinplate toys, which included animals, walking soldiers, clowns, and other figures. They were very successful, and the firm soon moved to larger premises. However, with the outbreak of the First World War the factory had to close, and the two partners went into military service. At the end of the War in 1918 the firm resumed production, but by this time Müller had a new partner, Adolph Kahn, and a new factory in Nuremberg. They registered the name Schuco as their trademark in 1921. Müller continued to produce his novelty and mechanical animals and bears, and in 1921 introduced the famous line of Yes/No bears. These bears made their first appearance at the Leipzig Spring Toy Fair in Germany, and continued in production throughout the firm's history, stopping only for a brief period during the Second World War. Other collectible and interesting lines include the Bellhop bear and miniature novelties in the form of compacts, perfume bottles, and lipstick holders (*see p.46-7*). Müller died in 1958, and his son, Werner, carried on the business. However, Schuco was unable to compete with the emerging Japanese toy industry, and in the 1970s was sold to another toy manufacturer, Dundee Combex Marx.

RIGHT Yes/No bears take their name from the fact that when the tail is turned from side to side the bear's head moves to say "no," and when it is moved up and down the head nods to say "yes." The bears were made in many sizes throughout the firm's history. Although Schuco Yes/No bears produced before the Second World War were made in a variety of colors, this 1930s blue bear with light tips is very rare. He is even more collectible because he is in such excellent condition—often the color has faded and remains strong only at the joints. Apart from his color, he is almost identical to the bear at the top of the opposite page, with close-set eyes and an upturned nose.
Height: 20in (51cm)
Approx value: $8,300

INSET After the Second World War mohair was very expensive, so manufacturers started to make dressed teddy bears with cotton bodies in order to save on fabric. Although Schuco produced many dressed bears in the 1950s, they are quite hard to find today. The Yes/No bear illustrated here was one of a pair, dressed as a Dutch boy and girl. His tail, which operates his head, is sticking out of his pants at the back so that it can be easily reached to move. He has the later plastic label on his chest with the word "Tricky" on it, introduced in 1953.
Height: 12in (30.5cm)
Approx value: $900

ABOVE This 1920s Yes/No has long cream mohair with distinct lilac tipping. He has the typical Schuco upturned nose. He still retains the original paper label on his chest.
Height: 17in (44cm)
Approx value: $6,800

LEFT This 1950s bear has the characteristic black and brown glass eyes and vertically stitched nose of Yes/No bears. Notable differences from earlier examples are the downward turning paws and longer, thinner limbs. He has the typically large flat feet which enable him to stand up. With their appealing, round faces these later Yes/No bears are very popular with collectors.
Height: 17in (43cm)
Approx value: $900

ABOVE The Bellhop bear, first made in 1921, was produced in many sizes. The bears are made of golden short bristle mohair and are dressed in felt clothes which cannot be removed. The largest shown here is a Yes/No bear from around 1923. He is in excellent condition, and still has his leather strap and bag—often this is missing. The smallest—not a Bellhop—is a dancing bear, who is operated by winding up a key.
Height: *left* 11in (25cm); *centre* 6in (15cm); *right* 4in (12cm)
Approx value: $1,500-4,500

ABOVE Googly-eyed Yes/No bears with open mouths and large round eyes, known as Baby-Bärs, were made by Schuco in the 1930s.
Height: *left* 11in (28cm); *right* 13in (33cm)
Approx value: $4,500-6,800

ABOVE Yes/No bears from the late 1950s/60s have the shaved muzzle and black nose stitching seen on this example. They also have shaved mohair on their feet, instead of felt pads.
Height: 20in (51 cm)
Approx value: $550

Schuco Miniatures

Schuco is particularly famous for its miniature and novelty toys, produced in vast numbers from the 1920s to the 1970s. The firm made a variety of clockwork and novelty animals which have great appeal to collectors today. Although their favorite subjects seem to have been mice and monkeys, they made all kinds of creatures. Many of the miniatures were made of tinplate covered in mohair—a combination exclusive to Schuco—but examples were also made in felt. The miniature teddy bears were made in many colors and are very collectible today. They included a line of novelty accessories for women, including bears concealing perfume bottles, bears that open up to reveal powder compacts, manicure sets, and miniature dice. Schuco also made a line of clockwork acrobatic and tumbling bears. In the 1930s Schuco introduced wooden cars called Rollers for their miniature animals to travel around in. The cars were made of metal, had three wheels, and were powered by a friction movement. On some examples the vehicles had wings so they could be converted to airplanes. These are very popular among collectors today. Of all the novelties, it is the rare colors that are most valuable.

LEFT Typically, the group of 1950s miniature bears shown here scrambling over a chair are truly tiny. However, despite their size they share the same close attention to detail and high quality as the larger bears, and are quite similar in style. Like most small teddy bears, none of these have paw pads (although those made in the 1920s did). Included in the group is the popular Berlin bear first made in the 1950s and produced by a number of manufacturers. Schuco made its miniatures bears in gold, cream, and red. They produced other miniature animals, and the small panda bear seen here. The large 1920s bear standing behind the chair in this picture is typical of Schuco's early Yes/No designs (*see previous page*), with a somewhat square head and downturned mouth that differs from that of the later Yes/No bears **Height:** *large bear* 20in (51cm); *minatures* 2 ½-5in (6.5-13cm) **Approx value:** *large bear* $1,200 plus; *miniatures* $130-680 each

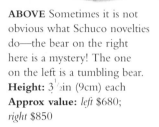

ABOVE These two Schucos are traveling around in their prestigious wooden Rollers! Although the drivers of the cars shown here are typical Schuco miniature bears, mice, chimpanzees, and even humans can sometimes be seen sitting at the wheel. Others, like the bear on the left, remained standing up. The metal vehicles are always stamped on the side with the Schuco trademark.
Height: 3^1/$_4$in (8cm)
Approx value: $900 each

ABOVE Sometimes it is not obvious what Schuco novelties do—the bear on the right here is a mystery! The one on the left is a tumbling bear.
Height: 3^1/$_2$in (9cm) each
Approx value: *left* $680; *right* $850

ABOVE This little bear from the 1950s is known as "Janus," because if you twist a knob at the base of his body his sweet face transforms into the evil-looking one on the right.
Height: 3^1/$_2$in (9cm)
Approx value: $600

ABOVE When the head of the bear on the left is removed the body opens to reveal a powder compact and a powder puff. The neck opening often held a lipstick. The most usual color is gold, but others were made in red and green—the mauve compact bear in the center is particularly rare. The popular bear on the right conceals a perfume bottle.
Height: 3^1/$_2$in (9cm) each
Approx value: $680-980 each

ABOVE By comparing the 1920s miniatures on the left with the 1950s group on the right it is possible to see changes in the design; the early bears are very small, are less rounded, have thinner limbs, and felt paw pads. Their stitched noses are very large in comparison to their bodies.
Height: *left pair* 2^1/$_2$in (6cm); *right pair* 3^1/$_2$in (9cm)
Approx value: *left pair* $350 each; *right pair* $180 each

SCHUCO ANIMALS

Schuco made a range of miniature animals, mechanical and non-mechanical, which are highly collectible today. They are all fully jointed and made of short mohair plush. Sizes vary from only 2 inches (5cm) to 3^1/$_2$ inches. Those shown here are only a small selection. The tiny chimp is the smallest animal they ever made. The monkey on the far left conceals a perfume bottle.

Monkey, c.1930   Chimp, c.1930   1930s rabbits   1950s rabbit   1950s lion

Musical Bears

A number of brightly colored long-haired bears which play a variety of jingly tunes when their tummies are squeezed have caused much debate among collectors about who made them. Although unmarked, these bears have the name "Helvetic" on the music box suggesting that the bears were all made by the same firm. In 1928 the U.S. trade magazine *Toy World* reported that Helvetic held the exclusive manufacturing rights to teddy bears with squeeze-operated music boxes. However, there is no evidence that such a factory existed, and it is increasingly likely that several toy manufacturers made the bears, with only the music boxes stamped "Helvetic". This theory is supported by evidence of a German manufacturer named Jopi that produced teddy bears previously thought to be made by Helvetic. Josef Pitrmann from Nüremberg was making toys as early as 1911, and in 1922 the trademarks "Bear with a Christmas Tree" and "Jopi" were registered. A Jopi brochure shows some of the bears which, together with pictures of a Jopi bear found recently with its label, mean that quite a few previously unidentified bears can now be attributed to this firm.

RIGHT AND ABOVE The exceptionally large Jopi on the right has a stitch attached to his chest where his tag would have been. He has the typical vertical nose stitching of Jopi's larger bears, which is almost identical to that used by Bing (*see p.36*). His glass eyes would originally have had painted backs but are now clear. It seems that Jopi also made non-musical bears, because the bear above, although virtually identical to the bear on the right, with large glass eyes set close together and round ears on the side of his head, does not have a musical mechanism in his body. **Height:** *right* 26in (66cm); *above* 24in (61cm) **Approx value:** *right* $9,800; *above* $5,300

RIGHT Although these two bears do not have Jopi labels they were almost certainly made by Jopi because they are virtually identical to the pink-frosted bear featured in their brochure. Features also found in that bear include long, slim, felt paw and foot pads cut slightly at an angle; three long stitched claws which do not run onto the felt; glass eyes with painted backs; large ears and long mohair. Like Steiff and Bing, Jopi seems to have used horizontal nose stitching on the smaller bears and vertical stitching for the larger ones. The musical mechanism is operated by a bellows movement inside the bear's tummy. Most are still in working order, and few play the same tune, so it is possible to build up quite a repertoire!
Height: 16in (40.6cm) each
Approx value: $3,000 each

LEFT This shocking-pink bear shows little resemblance to the others in this section, and it is possible he was made by a different factory. He has a very small horizontally stitched nose and an unusual straight mouth. His eyes are sewn through to the back of his head.
Height: 14in (35.5cm)
Approx value: $1,400

BELOW Several musical bears have appeared on the market with the distinctive bat-wing nose stitching seen on these two bears, so it is likely they were made by the same maker. Common features include the short velvet paw pads and long narrow foot pads cut slightly on the cross, glass eyes, and the absence of a mouth. The clown was originally lilac, but now only the joints show any color; his replacement ruff and hat are a faithful copy of the originals shown in the photograph of the bear with its owner. The bright color of the undressed bear makes him particularly desirable.
Height: 12in (30.5cm) each
Approx value: $2,300 each

LEFT These three bears demonstrate some of the other designs of musical bears that were made in Germany in the 1930s. The bear sitting on the piano has a shaved muzzle and a distinctive turned-up nose. The bear sitting on the floor has large eyes set far apart and claw stitching on his paws that continues over onto his pads. His pink hue has now faded. The bear leaning against the piano is made of short bristle mohair, a very unusual feature on musical examples. He is stuffed with wood wool, which makes his body very hard. Similarities between him and known Jopi bears include the long slim feet and the absence of claw stitching.
Height: 15in (38cm) each
Approx value: $2,700 each

Other German Makers

The city of Sonneberg in Germany was the center of soft toy production up until the Second World War. The city and surrounding villages were part of an intricate cottage industry producing dolls and plush or papier mâché toys. Many of these products were not labeled, and good-quality German bears often appear on the market with little supporting documentation, making them difficult to identify. In recent years new German factories have been discovered, and more information is gradually being gathered. Old catalogs and ads are particularly useful when trying to find out the makers of these unmarked bears. Several firms copied Steiff's designs, but perhaps none so blatantly as Strunz, who not only made direct copies of Steiff bears, but also used virtually identical advertising, and gave the bears a button-in-the-ear trademark just as Steiff did.

EDUARD CRÄMER

There is very little documented history about this German manufacturer of soft toys, although the bears have been known for a long time and are popular with collectors. A 1927 advertisement in a recently discovered German trade magazine states that the firm of Eduard Crämer, Schalkau, Thüringia, was established in 1896, and plush bears were an early feature of their line. Although unlabeled, these bears can be identified by their heart-shaped faces and open mouths, and through comparison with old ads. Eduard Crämer also made mechanical bears, and musical bears operated by moving the head backwards and forwards.

ABOVE Eduard Crämer's open-mouthed bears first appeared in the firm's 1930s ads. They have particularly long pronounced muzzles of clipped plush mohair. Some had light-brown nose stitching. Similar to a number of Hermann bears, they have a distinctive heart-shaped face.
Height: 15in (38cm)
Approx value: $2,300

RIGHT This bear has the distinctive button-hole mouth of many Crämer bears. Made around 1930, his golden mohair is now a bit sparse, but he still has lots of character. The feet are unusually long, of clipped mohair, with felt pads reinforced with cardboard.
Height: 13in (33cm)
Approx value: $900

LEFT This Strunz bear from around 1904 is virtually identical to Steiff's earliest rodded bear (*see p.22*). Common features with the Steiff bear include rod joints, black boot-button eyes, felt nose, pronounced humped back, and very long arms.
Height: 20¹⁄₂in (50cm)
Approx value: $1,500–3,000

STRUNZ

Wilhelm Strunz's Nuremberg-based factory made mohair bears as early as 1904, in direct and blatant competition with Steiff. Steiff fought bitterly with Strunz, particularly about the button-in-the-ear trademark, and in 1908 Strunz finally agreed to withdraw the button, instead securing a tag in the left ear with a staple. This was soon abandoned, and from 1910 the bears were marked with the word "Präsident." The side-by-side comparison of these elephants shows the similarities between the firms. The Strunz (*right*) is exactly the same shape as the Steiff.

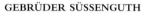

RIGHT This brown Peter Bear is the most common design. He had glass eyes, or—more often—the wooden ones seen here. The heads were made from cartons pressed into shape and stapled together, and the plush was glued on afterwards. They have movable eyes, open mouths, and wooden teeth.
Height: 14in (35.5cm)
Approx value: $5,300

GEBRÜDER SÜSSENGUTH

Very little is known about this East German toy manufacturer, apart from the fact that it was founded in Neustadt near Coburg, Thuringia, in 1894, and produced a variety of dolls and toys between 1925 and 1928. They are best known for their series of Peter bears. A hundred of these bears were discovered in a closed-down store in East Germany in 1974, and were brought over to England to be sold. Each pristine bear came in its original box, fully labeled, with a round tag on its chest with the words "*Peter, Ges Gesch* (legally protected)," and a serial number. These hundred examples seem to be the only ones that exist, and are therefore very rare. They were made in several sizes and different colors, and include a large pink bear, of which only two examples are known to exist. Gray and apricot Peter bears were also produced, but the brown example shown on the left here is the one most likely to be found on the market today.

RIGHT Although this bear does not have a label, he very closely resembles the musical bears made by Jopi (*see pp.48-9*). He is a novelty bear and has a zip down his back that opens to reveal a metal hot water bottle inside (shown here with the bear).
Height: 25in (63.5cm)
Approx value: $5,300

IDENTIFYING A GERMAN BEAR

Sometimes the only way to identify a bear is by comparing it with similar examples with their original tags, or with those featured in old ads.
German characteristics include:
•a wide round head
•a long muzzle
•long realistic limbs
•a humped back
•high quality long German mohair
The two bears on the right have labels saying they were made in East Germany, but there is no mention of the maker.

British Bears

The British followed quickly on the heels of the Germans and the Americans in the production of teddy bears (although some British collectors maintain the teddy bear was a British invention, named after King Edward VII, whose nickname was "Teddy"). Early manufacturers, such as J.K. Farnell, had been making toys since the 19th century, so when the teddy bear craze hit Britain they were easily able to switch to making bears. Bans on imports from Germany during the First World War led to more British bear manufacturers setting up factories, including Harwin & Co., Chad Valley, Chiltern, William J. Terry, and Dean's, and these early bears are all very collectible.

Early British bears are of very high quality, and are usually made from Yorkshire mohair plush. Post-Second World War examples are quite different in style, with the flat face, plump body, and short limbs that are now regarded as typical features of an English bear. Identification of early bears is difficult, as many have no labels, but comparing them with old company ads can help.

LEFT A Merrythought Cheeky, a Chiltern, and a Chad Valley bear enjoying a train journey.

RIGHT A Peacock bear with his arm around a Chad Valley.

J.K. Farnell

J.K. Farnell was one of the first companies to make bears. In fact, some have suggested that they made the first teddy bear, even before Steiff, and although this has not been proven, it is almost certain they made bears in the early years of the 20th century. The family business was established in 1840 in Notting Hill, London, by John Farnell, initially making small items such as pin cushions. Following John's death in 1897 his children, Agnes and Henry, relocated to Acton and set up a soft toy business there using rabbit skins. In 1921 Agnes set up the Alpha Works next to the existing Farnell factory. She produced teddy bears with the designer Sybil Kemp, and in 1925 they registered the Alpha trademark for all Farnell bears. Among the British outlets selling Alpha bears was the famous London department store, Harrods, where the original Alpha Winnie the Pooh bear is said to have been bought for the young Christopher Robin (*see pp.148-9*). Very few early bears have been found with Farnell labels, and many can be attributed to Farnell only by their similarity in style to the later Alpha range. Farnell continued to produce bears until the 1960s, but their early designs are the most desirable.

RIGHT This bear closely resembles the Alpha bear bought for Christopher Robin in 1921. He probably dates from around 1918, before the Farnell design was officially registered as an Alpha. One of the most notable characteristics of Farnell bears is the wonderful quality of the mohair, which is always long and silky, and this bear's golden mohair is no exception. The long, shaved muzzle is typical of that found on early Farnell bears. This bear has the distinctive webbed claw stitching often used by Farnell until the 1930s. Other British manufacturers such as W. J. Terry also used webbed claw stitching, but their nose stitching was different.
Height: 28in (71cm)
Approx value: $2,700-3,800

LEFT Documentary evidence is very useful when trying to date early Farnell bears. This photograph can be dated to 1914, which means that the bear the little girl is holding also dates from around that year. The bear is known to be a Farnell, and comparing other bears with this one will help to determine when they were made too.

RIGHT Some early Farnell bears have the slightly upturned noses of the two examples shown here. It is not certain whether this design was made at the same time as the others featured on this page, or at a slightly later date. Typically, the smaller bear has no stitching on his paw pads. **Height:** *large* 25in (63cm); *small* 13in (33cm) **Approx value:** *large* $3,300; *small* $900-1,200

BELOW The bright red color of this early Farnell bear is very rare. Like Steiff bears, he has a definite hump on his back. His exceptionally shiny black button eyes are a distinctive feature of Farnell's early bears. However, Farnell also made bears at this time with matte black button eyes. **Height:** 13in (33cm) **Approx value:** $1,200-1,500

ABOVE Similarities between this bear and the one in the photograph at the top of the page date him to around 1914. He is in excellent condition and there are no signs of wear on his coat. He has even managed to retain his original paw pads, which quite often are missing. **Height:** 16in(40.5cm) **Approx value:** $1,500-1,800

ABOVE It is unusual to find blond Farnells, and it is possible that this bear has simply discolored, and was originally white. He is another popular early Farnell design. Although still chubby when viewed from the front, his body is rather flat and he does not have a hump on his back. The tops of his arms are very plump. He has replacement paw pads, but they have been made in the style of the originals and will not detract too much from the value. **Height:** 26in (66cm) **Approx value:** $1,800-2,700

BELOW It is rare to find three white Farnells together in such perfect condition as these bears, all dating from around 1920. The two on the right have been in the possession of a family in Scotland for years.

It is always a good idea to carefully remove any replacement paw pads on Farnell bears to see what is behind. When the pads of the biggest bear were removed the owner found that he still had all the original claw stitching underneath! The bear in the middle has a horizontal stitch across his chest where his paper label would have been (see Jemima Puddleduck's paper label on p.59).
Height: *left* 23in (58cm); *right* 16in (40.5cm); *front* 12in (30.5cm)
Approx value: *left* $2,700–3,000; *right* $1,800–2,300; *front* $1,200–1,400

TYPICAL FEATURES OF PRE-1930s FARNELL BEARS

•long, plump arms

•shaved muzzle

•vertical nose stitching

•glossy mohair coat

•large ears

•plump body

•back hump

•webbed claw stitching (not on smaller bears)

•cardboard inserts in the feet

Black webbed stitching used on pre-1930 Farnell bears.

LEFT Several examples of the bear on the left have appeared in recent years. Although he is different in many ways from the typical Farnell bear–he has very large glass eyes, does not have the Farnell nose, and his body is longer–when placed next to one it is clear he is by the same maker because his silky mohair coat and plump limbs are distinctive Farnell traits. **Height:** 25in (63.5cm) **Approx value:** $2,400-2,700

Some bears from 1915 until the 1930s have clear glass eyes with black pupils.

This type of nose was a feature of early bears until the 1930s.

BELOW These two bears have the webbed paw stitching used by Farnell until 1930. After that time the same type of stitching appeared on Merrythought bears, as

Farnell's designer transferred there in that year (*see p.69*). **Height:** *left* 20in (51cm); *right* 15in (38cm) **Approx value:** $2,300-2,900 each

This very shiny black button eye is an alternative design on early Farnell bears.

White Farnell bears had the brown stitching seen in this photograph.

Brown and black glass eyes were used from around 1915 onwards.

By the 1930s Farnell noses were squarer and no longer had the long end-stitches.

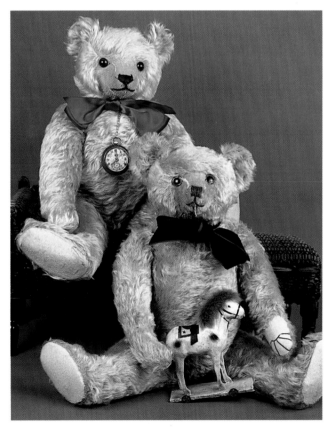

The remains of the original paint can be seen on this glass eye.

After the Second World War the nose became more bulbous.

Farnell produced this Beatrix Potter children's story character, Jemima Puddleduck, in 1925. Made of white mohair, she is in mint condition and still retains her original paisley cotton shawl and blue bonnet. She also has the origi-nal paper tag with metal around the edge that was used by Farnell on their bears from 1925 (*see p.59*). Often this is missing, leaving a large stitch across the chest where the label was attached.
Height: 12in (30.5cm)
Approx value: $750-900

FARNELL ANIMALS

Farnell produced a wide range of animals using the same attention to detail and high quality materials as they did for their teddy bears. Most people buying toy animals do so to complement their bear collection, because bears look very attractive displayed with fellow companions. A number of Farnell animals, like the elephant and Jemima Puddleduck shown here, were dressed. Farnell also made a range of felt dolls, which are highly collectible; perhaps the most famous of these are their dolls modeled as the British kings Edward VIII and George VI, made in the late 1930s.

This monkey is made of long, white mohair. He has felt hands and feet, and a smiling face of pressed felt. His human-like brown and white glass eyes are particularly unusual, and quite different from the eyes used on Farnell bears. Made in 1930, he is still in perfect condition.
Height: 16in (41cm)
Approx value: $600-750

This charming Alpha elephant was made around 1935. His paw pads and felt clothes are all original and in good condition. Only the visible areas are mohair; his body is cotton.
Height: 15in (38cm)
Approx Value: $450

RIGHT Unshaven muzzles were popular on Farnell's Alpha bears from around 1926 onwards. This bear is quite different from earlier examples, and has large glass eyes and a square nose. The later paw stitching, which is no longer webbed, is clearly visible. Long stitches now go from the top of the fabric on the feet over onto the felt. A blue and white embroi-dered label sewn onto the foot was introduced around this time.
Height: 20in (51cm)
Approx value: $2,300-2,600

ABOVE A number of Farnell's later Alpha bears have particularly long mohair coats. This example from the 1930s has a very different face from the earlier bears; his muzzle is no longer shaved or pronounced, and his nose is a solid block and has more definite stitching. Bears from this time are now easy to date and recognize because Farnell started sewing labels onto the bear's foot in 1925.
Height: 13in (33cm)
Approx value: $1,200–1,400

ABOVE Along with other British teddy bear manufacturers, Farnell produced a number of colored plush bears in the 1930s. These are particularly rare and collectible today. However, the relatively poor condition of this bear will reduce its value. His eyes are now clear, because the original black paint has worn off. The long mohair coats of Farnell bears have very rarely worn thin.
Height: 13in (33cm)
Approx value: $750–900

ABOVE Farnell changed the design of their Alpha bears following the total destruction of their stock by fire in 1934. They opened a new factory in 1935 and relaunched the Alpha label. This Alpha bear from around 1938 has brown and black glass eyes, a shorter nose, and smaller ears than pre-1943 examples. His limbs are much slimmer and do not have curved paws. He still has the embroidered label on his foot.
Height: 13in (33cm)
Approx value: $400–700

ABOVE After the Second World War Farnell produced bears with vivid red or blue paw pads, which gave the bears a somewhat comical appearance. Typical of post-Second World War bears, this one has a very small body in proportion to the size of his head, and his limbs and feet are short. He still has his original label, printed in a shield design. The pale stitching was often used on Farnell's white bears.
Height: 13in (33cm)
Approx value: $300–450

Paper tag used up until 1925

Embroidered label, 1925–c.1945

Alternative label, 1925–45

Printed label used from the 1940s

ABOVE Although this looks like a later Farnell bear, he has no label and it is possible that he was made by the British manufacturer, Invicta, (*see p.79*), whose bears had many similar characteristics.
Height: 13in (33cm)
Approx value: $150–300

Dean's Rag Book Co.

Dean's Rag Book Company was founded by Henry Samuel Dean in 1903, and is one of the oldest surviving toy companies in Britain. The firm started off making the now-famous range of indestructible rag books for children, and it was not until 1915 that the first teddy bears were introduced. Large-scale production of bears did not really begin until the 1920s. Dean's has always been well known for dolls; the bears were made in far fewer numbers, and are quite hard to find today. Most of those that survive date from the 1930s, Dean's most productive period before the austerity of the Second World War. At this time the factory was based in Merton, South London. After the War, business almost ceased, and it took a long time for the company to recover, especially because synthetic materials led to greater competition from elsewhere. The Merton factory was sold in 1955 and production moved to Rye, Sussex. In 1972 Dean's merged with Gwentoys in Pontypool, Wales, and from this time toys were produced in both factories. In 1988 a new Dean's company was formed. Dean's is re-establishing itself as a name in the teddy bear world, and has recently launched a whole new line of bears for collectors. It is also producing modern replicas of their old bears.

RIGHT This 1930s bear is known as the "mouse-eared" bear because he has a very round face and flat, wide-apart ears. His mohair coat was originally pink, but has now faded, with only hints of color still visible at the joints. He has glass eyes, a vertically stitched nose, and cream felt pads on his paws and feet. His head is stuffed with wood wool, and his body with kapok. His label is missing, but there are holes where it was sewn on.
Height: 18in (45cm)
Approx value: $600-700

ABOVE When London Zoo's first polar bear, Brumas, was born in 1949, Dean's produced this mohair version of mother Ivy holding her cub. It is very unusual to find the bears together, particularly with their paper labels.
Height: 19in (48cm)
Approx value: $900

ABOVE Although this 1936 bear has a narrow muzzle and his eyes are close together, he is still very simiiar to the bear on p.60, with the same round, smiling face, but of gold mohair rather than pink.
Height: 16in (40cm)
Approx value: $550–700

ABOVE This 1958 bear is in excellent condition. He has the typical flat face of Dean's later bears, with a shaved muzzle and high forehead. The bear was made in two colors, London gold and rich cedar.
Height: 24in (61cm)
Approx value: $400

BELOW Walt Disney's Mickey Mouse was produced by Dean's in around 1932. His googly eyes (celluloid eyes with a loose pupil) date him to this time. He was made at the Dean's Elephant and Castle factory in the East End of London, where toys were made from 1910 to 1936. He is very rare, and is in exceptional condition. The Dean's rag book is a "Funny ABC" book. It is a particularly early example, produced in 1912, and this, together with the fact that it is in excellent condition, make it highly collectible. The artist was G.H. Dodd.
Height: *Mickey Mouse* 8in (20cm); *rag book* 8in (20cm)
Approx value: *Mickey Mouse* $1,100; *rag book* $150

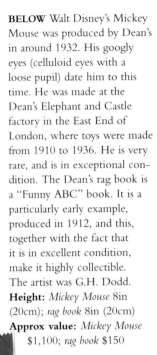

LEFT This black bear would originally have had claws molded out of latex, but these perished and have been replaced with felt pads. Designed in the 1950s, he is quite different from Dean's other bears. He was based on a real bear, and has an unjointed floppy body, glass eyes set in rubber sockets, a cream muzzle, and a large rubber nose.
Height: 19in (48cm)
Approx value: $850

LEFT Dean's are particularly famous for their dolls. They produced a vast range, many modeled on famous characters taken from childrens' stories and nursery rhymes, as well as famous British performers such as George Robey, Arthur Askey, Stanley Lupino Lane, and many others. It is believed that only one hundred examples of this Yeoman of the Guard doll were made, for the coronation of King George VI in 1937. His face is made of pressed felt, and the eyes are hand-painted. He is filled with cotton waste or "sub" (substitute), a firm but less expensive alternative to kapok. This doll is an excellent example in pristine condition, and will command a premium.
Height: 16in (40cm)
Approx value: $1,200 in mint condition

ABOVE This popular bear first appeared in 1938, but remained in production until the 1950s, and quite a few have survived today. He has a triangular face and small ears set at the corner of his head. His eyes are black and brown plastic.
Height: 28in (71cm)
Approx value: $600–750

ABOVE Dean's introduced lock-in safety eyes for their nursery toys in the early 1950s, but did not extend this to its bears until the late 1950s. They embarked on a safety campaign in the 1960s, making all their bears suitable for children.
Height: 24in (61cm)
Approx value: $400

Printed cloth label used from the 1920s-55

Dean's label used on Beefeater doll, 1937

Paper swing tag used between 1937 and 1955

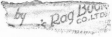

MUSiCAL
DEAN'S CHILDSPLAY TOYS LTD
RYE · SUSSEX

from 1956

1950s paper tag

Printed Childsplay label, used from 1956 to the 1980s, when the factory moved to Rye

DEAN'S

1986-91

Printed and paper label used from 1960-70

1968 swing tag holding a spare safety lock-in eye, introduced in that year

BELOW Dean's made a number of musical bears after the Second World War. This example was made in 1961 at the factory in Rye. Although he has a mohair body, his paw pads are synthetic. The musical mechanism is worked by turning the key located at the back of his body. Like a number of Dean's later bears, this one has a large triangular head and a flat face.
Height: 16in (40cm)
Approx value: $550

RIGHT Bears have been increasingly associated with romance over the years and many bear cards and products have been produced for this market. This synthetic fiber bear was specially produced for Valentines Day in 1980, and has been dressed with a special bow with hearts on it. He was made at the Pontypool factory in Wales, home of Gwentoys, bought by Dean's in 1972.
Height: 16in (40cm)
Approx value: $150

ABOVE Dean's designer Sylvia Willgoss created this large, rich brown bear in the 1970s, based on the bears in London Zoo. He is made of synthetic non-flammable hair with black safety eyes and polyurethane stuffing. Like most of her designs, he is unjointed. He also comes in rich gold and in black, and in three sizes.
Height: 30in (80cm)
Approx value: $400

LEFT Later Dean's bears were filled with chipped foam. This bear, made in 1965, is in mint condition and has all his original labels. His eyes are plastic, but his body is mohair. He has the characteristic triangular head of later bears.
Height: 16in (40cm)
Approx value: $150

FAR RIGHT Dean's recently launched a Collectors Club line of bears aimed at the collector's market: they have all been designed to re-create the traditional characteristics of Dean's early bears. The three shown here featured in the 1994 catalog. Hector in the middle is made in distressed straw-colored mohair and is fully jointed. He was given to each member upon joining the Club. George, on the left, is made of antique gold long pile mohair, and Amy on the right is made of thick pile gray/blue mohair.
Height: *left* 10in (26cm); *center* 12in (30cm); *right* 9in (23cm)
Approx value: $75 plus each

Chad Valley

Chad Valley began as a printing business in Birmingham in 1820, run by Joseph and Alfred Johnson under the name of Johnson Bros. Ltd. The factory moved to new premises in Harborne in 1897 and registered Chad Valley as its trademark after the Chad stream that ran nearby. The brothers produced their first bears in 1915, inspired by the ban on imports of bears to Britain. Chad Valley was soon making a variety of soft toys and bears, and in 1920 it moved to the site of the Wrekin Toy Works in Shropshire, taking over the works and forming the present Chad Valley Co. Ltd. The firm continued to expand, introducing new bears and novelty items. In 1938 they were granted Royal Warrant of Appointment as Toymakers to Her Majesty the Queen, a warrant that continued until Elizabeth II became Queen, when the warrant stayed with her as Queen Mother. Production flourished after the Second World War, but in the 1970s Chad's business declined. In 1978 they were taken over by Palitoy, and in 1988 the British chain store Woolworths adopted the Chad name.

LEFT These two bears from the 1930s show the two types of early Chad Valley nose. The smaller bear on the right has the vertically stitched triangular nose used only on earlier examples, whereas the larger bear has the coal-shaped nose that was soon to become the standard design. Typical Chad Valley characteristics include large flat ears set wide apart on the head, amber and black glass eyes, shaved muzzle, and large, oval paw pads with cardboard inserts. **Height:** *left* 21in (53cm); *right* 17in (43cm) **Approx value:** $700–1,000 each

RIGHT Chad Valley produced a number of novelty toys and animals, including Disney characters and the famous Sooty puppet (*see p. 67*). They made this popular cartoon dog, Bonzo, in several different designs and sizes. Steiff also made a version, but it was not very popular (*see p. 29*). This Bonzo from around 1930 is in particularly fine condition, because the airbrushed features have not faded. His body is made of velvet and stuffed with kapok. He has a leather collar and red felt tongue.
Height: 14in (35.5cm)
Approx value: $550–1,000

ABOVE The pristine condition of this small gold mohair bear is amazing considering he was made in the 1930s. He even has his original ribbon and label. It is rare to find such an early bear with its label, especially in perfect condition.
Height: 13in (33cm)
Approx value: $700–1,200

ABOVE A very different design was the Magna bear, produced in the 1930s. Identifying features include small wide-set ears, an unshaved muzzle, and a narrow rectangular nose with horizontal stitching.
Height: 15in (38cm)
Approx value: $400–700

1930s button

1930s button

Earliest button

Chad Valley Magna nose, 1930s

Typical post-1945 Chad Valley nose

Standard "coal-shaped" nose, 1930s onwards

RIGHT The label on this bear's right paw bears the words "Toymakers to Her Majesty the Queen," which dates the bear to between 1938 and 1952. The bear was a popular Chad design and was produced in large quantities. Because these bears are not difficult to find today, it is worth looking for one in good condition. The felt paw pads of earlier years have by the time of this bear been replaced with rexine ones, and on this example they are somewhat worn. Other bears from this time have the velvet pads seen on the next page. An identical bear to this was made with shaggy mohair.
Height: 25in (63.5cm)
Approx value: $550–850

RIGHT The large flat ears and chunky, jointed limbs of this bear are characteristic of Chad Valley bears made after the Second World War. The fact that the label on this bear states that he was made under Royal Warrant to the Queen Mother dates it to after 1953, when Elizabeth II was crowned

Queen and the label was changed to say "Queen Mother" (*see the labels on p.67*). This bear has a black stitched nose and glass eyes, but many other examples had plastic safety noses and plastic eyes at this time.
Height: 28in (71cm)
Approx value: $700–1,000

RIGHT This group of bears from the 1950s can be instantly identified as Chad Valley by the abundance of paper labels. The bears' eyes are plastic, and they have black-stitched button noses instead of the earlier bound examples. Although some bears produced after the Second World War were made of nylon, these three have mohair coats and velvet pads. These particular bears were among a number used by Bear Brand Stockings to advertise their products, and because they were used for display purposes and have never been played with, they are in excellent condition.
Height: *back bear* 43in (109cm); *front left* 27in (68.5cm); *front right* 27in (68.5cm)
Approx value: $550–900 each

ABOVE This bear is very similar in shape to the one next to it, but he looks different because he has been given replacement eyes that are too small for the size of his head. His mohair coat is still very fluffy and his paw pads are in good condition.
Height: 17in (43cm)
Approx value: $400–700

LEFT Chad Valley bears such as this one made after the Second World War had much shorter limbs than earlier examples and their bodies were less plump. Although this example is made of mohair, Chad also made bears in a variety of less expensive synthetic fabrics at this time and in many different colors. **Height:** 15in (38cm) **Approx value:** $150-300

ABOVE Toffee bear was a popular British radio character in the 1950s, and both Chad Valley and Farnell made soft toy versions of him. This example has lost his original woolen hat and scarf, but is in otherwise excellent condition. **Height:** 10in (25cm) **Approx value:** $350-550

1930s embroidered label

1938-53 foot label and chest tag

Post-coronation (1953) foot label

1950s blue printed chest label

1920s Chad Valley doll label

Paper label used on bears in the 1930s

LEFT In addition to teddy bears, Chad Valley produced a variety of different animals, famous characters, and felt dolls (which included the popular Mabel Lucie-Attwell doll made in the 1920s), to meet with competition from other toy manufacturers. Like a number of other British manufacturers, including Merrythought, Chad started producing pandas after the first panda was introduced to London Zoo. This large panda bear has the same shaved muzzle and horizontal nose stitching as the Magna bear (*see p.65*). **Height:** 20in (51cm) **Approx value:** $300-600

RIGHT Chad Valley was given the sole right to manufacture British comedian Harry Corbett's glove puppet Sooty in 1952, and they continued producing it until 1980. The first Sooty was purchased by Corbett from an old lady on Blackpool pier. Corbett blackened the nose and ears with soot, hence the now famous name. No one knows where the first Sooty is, but it is estimated that over a thousand puppets have been worn out in the shows since that time. **Height:** 9in (23cm) **Approx value:** $120-250

Merrythought

In 1919 W.G. Holmes went into partnership with G.H. Laxton and opened a small spinning mill in Oakworth, Yorkshire. They took over a weaving factory in Huddersfield in 1920 and hired as directors Mr. A.C. Janisch, previously sales director at J.K. Farnell, and Mr. C.J. Rendle, previously in charge of toy production at Chad Valley. Consequently, the influences of both Chad and Farnell can be seen in Merrythought bears. In 1930, the company rented premises from Coalbrookdale in Shropshire, which they later purchased, and from which they still work today. They registered as Merrythought Ltd. in the same year, taking their name from the old 17th-century English word for wishbone, the symbol of good luck that appears on the button and label of their bears.

Merrythought is one of the leading British soft toy manufacturers and their bears are eagerly sought-after by collectors. Up until the Second World War bears were made with both a paper label and a metal button on the inside of the left ear, and although the label is often missing, most bears still have their buttons. Because the bears are well documented, widely available, and made in a variety of designs, they are ideal to collect. Popular designs include the dressed Bingie bears and the Cheeky bears.

RIGHT With the exception of the Cradle Bingie, which was made after the Second World War, Merrythought produced its Bingie line of bears between 1931 and 1938. These dressed bears came as a sitting cub (undressed), Baby Bingie, Cutie Bingie, Girl, Boy, Grenadier Guardsman, Sailor, Ski-Girl, and Highlander. Today Bingies are very rare, particularly if they have their original clothes. Undressed Bingies can also be found on the market. This Highlander Bingie from around 1925 is in particularly fine condition. Typically, his ears are lined with white art silk plush. These bears' undressed bodies are made of brushed cotton, and as can be seen in the inset picture, only the visible parts are made of mohair.
Height: 20in (46cm)
Approx value: $2,700

RIGHT Bobby Bruin was first made in 1936, in three sizes, with movable joints: metal rods were passed through the legs and ended in rings around the feet that enabled the bear to take up many positions. He is quite different from the usual Merrythought bear, having been designed to look more realistic. He does not have a shaved muzzle and his nose does not have the usual drop stitches. His ears placed flat at the side of his head make him look like a dog.
Height: 26in (66 cm)
Approx value: $1,200

Bobby Bruin's nose, an alternative 1936 design

The typical down-stitched nose of Merrythought bears

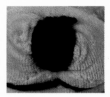

The pinched Cheeky nose, used from 1957 onwards

The influence of Farnell's director is most evident in the distinctive webbed claw stitching, which was a feature on Farnell bears until he left the company to join Merrythought in 1930.

Both types of stitching were used on paws from the 1930s

LEFT British toymakers first produced soft toy pandas after panda bears were introduced to London Zoo. Merrythought made their first panda bear in 1937, and continues to make them today. This example is one of the company's largest. Although he is a bit dirty, his face is expressive. An unusual feature is the leather claws on either paw. His nose is horizontally stitched and is quite unlike the usual Merry-thought nose.
Height: 23in (58cm)
Approx value: $550

ABOVE Colored bears were popular with manufacturers throughout the 1930s, but unfortunately few have managed to retain their bright hues. It is particularly surprising that this Merrythought bear should still be quite dark, as blue is the color most likely to fade. He has the clipped muzzle, webbed claw stitching, and felt pads of many Merrythought bears, and the typical black nose with dropped stitching.
Height: 19in (45.5cm)
Approx value: $1,000

ABOVE Production of bears virtually ceased during the Second World War because all efforts were needed for muni-tions. Bears made afterwards changed little, although the button in the ear was no longer used, and the label was printed, not embroidered. This bear from around 1950 has many of the typical features of pre-War examples. This claw stitching was used simultaneously with the webbed type seen on other bears shown on these pages.
Height: 19in (45.5cm)
Approx value: $750

BELOW This unusual "Punkinhead" bear was specially made by Merrythought for Eatons department store in Canada in 1949 as a rival to Rudolph the Reindeer promoted by a nearby store. The "bear" was used as their mascot until 1956, and participated in a number of Christmas parades through the streets. The most distinctive feature is probably his white mohair topknot. The bears had sewn-on felt pants in green, yellow, red, or blue. Sometimes these have faded, and often are missing altogether. The pronounced shaved muzzle, smiling face, ears set at the side, and domed head make him an obvious forerunner of the Cheeky bear below.
Height: 16in (40.5cm)
Approx value: $1,200

RIGHT Mr. and Mrs. Twisty Cheeky, made between 1966 and 1988, have an internal wire that enables them to be twisted into different poses. It is rare to find the couple still together today.
Height: 11in (28cm)
Approx value: $1,300 pair

RIGHT Merrythought's Cheeky bear was introduced in 1957 and is still made today (*see the replica on p.120*)–this example from around 1960 is typical. Cheeky was so popular when he was brought out that many different versions were made, all with bells in their ears.
Height: 25in (63.5cm)
Approx value: $900

LEFT Clearly based on the earlier Bingie bears is the series of dressed London Bears made between 1972 and 1975. The line included a Guardsman, a Beefeater, a Highlander, and the Policeman shown here. At 36 inches (91.5cm) high this Policeman is particularly tall. Sizes usually ranged from 18 inches (46cm) to 30 inches (76cm). He still has his original paper label. Only his head, paws, and arms are mohair; the rest of his body is felt, making up part of his outfit. His ears have been set particularly low on his head so his hat can fit. To complete the character he carries a metal whistle. Dressed bears with all their accessories and clothes are extremely rare.
Height: 36in (91.5cm)
Approx value: $1,300

Metal button, 1930–45

Bobby Bruin label, 1936

Embroidered label, 1945–56

Paper label, used on the London Bears

Printed label, 1957–91

RIGHT Merrythought produced a vast range of animals, both domestic and wild. This smiling lion is just one of several different lions made by the firm.
Height: 14in (35.5cm)
Approx value: $120

LEFT Merrythought produces new designs of its Cheeky bears today, including special editions. The early Cheekys were made either of mohair or art silk plush, but modern examples can be either acrylic or mohair. These four modern Micro Cheeky bears appear in Merrythought's 1995 catalog, and were produced in a limited edition of only 500 each. Although tiny, they capture all the qualities of earlier, larger examples. A number of Cheekys were dressed—Bed-Time Cheeky has removable pajamas, robe, and slippers!
Height: 6in (15cm) each
Approx value: $75 each plus

Chiltern

In 1908 Joseph Eisenmann opened the Chiltern Toy Works at Chesham in Buckinghamshire. The works started by producing dolls, but in 1915 made their first bear, the Master Teddy. When Joseph died in 1919, he left the factory to his son-in-law, Leon Rees. A year later Leon moved to larger premises at Waterside in Chesham, and in partnership with Harry Stone formed H.G. Stone and Co. Ltd. A second factory was opened in Tottenham, London, in 1921. The Hugmee range of bears was introduced in 1923, and the name Chiltern Toys was registered in 1924. During the Second World War production ceased at Chesham, but continued at Tottenham. Afterwards, soft toy manufacturing moved to Amersham, Bucks, where it continued until the factory's closing in 1960. A second toy factory was opened at Pontypool in Wales in 1947. Chiltern was taken over by Chad Valley in 1967, and for a time bears bore a Chad Valley/Chiltern label.

Chiltern bears are very popular with collectors. Their high quality means many of them have survived, and usually in good condition. Hugmee bears were made in such a variety of patterns that it is possible to build up an interesting collection from these alone. Other collectible Chilterns include some of the novelty bears, such as the skater and the bear on a bike featured on these pages.

RIGHT Chiltern's earliest bear, the Master Teddy, was first produced in 1915 at the Chiltern Toy Works in Chesham. He was made in five sizes. The bears are dressed and only the visible parts are mohair—the rest of the body is made of cotton. Although the jacket on this example is old, it is not the original (but his trousers with a red patch are). He would have had a pink-and-white striped shirt with a white collar when he was made, but this is now missing, as is his paper label printed with his name. Master Teddy has a round head, and unlike Chiltern's other bears, has no muzzle. He has large googly eyes, a black-stitched nose, and a red tongue. He has no pads on his paws, but felt ones on his feet. Master Teddy is very rare today.
Height: 10in (25cm)
Approx value: $2,500

LEFT During the 1930s most British soft toy manufacturers produced bears in colored mohair. However, the pink-and -green color combination of this Hugmee bear is extremely unusual, and the fact that the bear is in such a good unfaded condition makes it an even more desirable collector's item. He has the characteristic long shaved muzzle and drumstick legs of early Chiltern designs.
Height: 10in (25.5cm)
Approx value: $825-1,275

ABOVE Chiltern made a number of different Hugmee designs. This 1930s bear does not have the shaved muzzle of many early bears. Also, his limbs are shorter, and his feet are smaller, and are not backed with cardboard.
Height: 16in (40.5cm)
Approx value: $450-750

ABOVE The pink plush of this 1930s Hugmee bear has managed to maintain its bright color despite its age.
Height: 16in (40.5cm)
Approx value: $520-825

Early Master Teddy nose

Early nose, 1920s–30s

Later nose, 1940–60s

Black plastic nose used on some 1960s Hugmee bears

ABOVE The pale color of the stitching on the nose and claws of this 1930s blond Hugmee bear make an otherwise typical bear unusual. Chiltern's early Hugmees were made in golden mohair as well as in a range of pastels, which included blue, pink, white, and green. As with many Chiltern bears, the eyes on this example are attached by a stitch tied in a knot at the back of the head. Even though this is quite a large bear, he is fairly light in weight, because his body is stuffed with kapok and his head with wood wool. He has the characteristic upturned paws of Chiltern bears.
Height: 28in (71cm)
Approx value: $975-1,450

ABOVE This 1935 gold mohair Hugmee bear has the typical face of Chiltern bears made before the Second World War, with a shaved muzzle and two long stitches either side of the nose. These bears have chubby drumstick-shaped thighs with tapering ankles.
Height: 20in (51cm)
Approx value: $450-825

LEFT This 1950s musical bear still has his paper label bearing the instructions. Unusually, this bear has its original blue ribbon. The flatter face is typical of later Hugmees, as is the stitching on the feet— the claws are now grouped together in sets of two.
Height: 16in (40.5cm)
Approx value: $675-975

ABOVE A new Hugmee pattern that used less fabric than earlier examples was added to the Chiltern lines after the Second World War. The arms and legs became much shorter, the faces flatter, and pads were made of rexine. This bear from around 1950 shows how the nose stitching has now changed to a shield shape without the longer stitches on either side. The downturned mouth gives him a somewhat serious expression. His sharply pointed feet are a distinctive Chiltern feature. The clothes belonged to a small child contemporary with the bear, and have been put on to protect the body from suffering excessive wear.
Height: 20in (51cm)
Approx value: $525-825

1930s label from the skater bear's foot

Printed label introduced in the 1950s

1950s musical bear label

ABOVE Chiltern first made this highly sought after artificial silk plush skater bear in the 1930s. This early example still has his label. He is in good condition: often the fur has faded or the muffs are missing.
Height: 11in (28cm)
Approx value: $750-800

LEFT Pam Howells designed this popular "Bear on a Trike" for Chiltern around 1958. Although only attached to his bike by stitching, he seems to manage never to fall off!
Height: 11in (28cm)
Approx value: $525-675

Bear type/date	Muzzle	Eyes	Nose	Limbs	Paws and pads	Label
1920s Hugmee	Unshaved pointed muzzle	Clear glass	Black-stitched with two long stitches going up at each end	Chubby drumstick-shaped thighs and long arms	Velvet/cotton, four claws	No printed label. Orange, circular paper tag, often missing
1930s Hugmee	Long shaved muzzle	Clear glass or amber and black			Velvet, four stitched claws	
1940s Hugmee	Flat face, short unshaved muzzle	Black and amber glass	Black-stitched shield-shaped	Short limbs, small feet and hands	Rexine, two sets of two stitches on feet	New printed label introduced
1950s/60s Hugmee	Long unshaved muzzle	Amber and black glass, sewn in the back of head	Black-stitched shield-shaped	Thick thighs, long arms	Four claws grouped together, five on feet	Printed label

LEFT This Tingaling Bruin bear from around 1953 is one of a range of musical bears made by Chiltern after the Second World War. The mechanism inside the body produces a musical tinkling sound when the bear is moved (other musical bears had bellows or, like the one on the previous page, were operated by turning a key). The shaved feet on this bear are similar to those designed by Steiff for their Teddy Babies. Quite different in appearance from earlier Hugmees, this bear has a shorter body, large feet, and small wide-apart ears: the nose is still shield-shaped.
Height: 15in (38cm)
Approx value: $375-675

ABOVE Some Hugmee bears made in the 1960s had black plastic noses, reputedly taken from toy dogs that were being made in the factory at the same time: the doggy expression of this bear is typical. The velveteen paw pads now have four stitched claws grouped together on the hands. The eyes are made of brown glass.
Height: 16in (40.5cm)
Approx value: $400-720

Back and front of a 1950s paper label

LEFT AND ABOVE This exceptionally large bear, *left*, from around 1958 has managed to keep its life-long companion, the shaggy dog, *above*. The bear's golden mohair plush is in excellent condition and he still has his original label, price tag, and ribbon. The floppy ears are characteristic of those on bears made after the Second World War. This bear still has glass eyes, but eyes were soon all to be replaced by plastic.
Height: *bear* 27in (68.7cm); *dog* 7in (18cm)
Approx value: $975-1,400 the pair

Pedigree Soft Toys Ltd.

Pedigree Soft Toys is a subsidiary of Lines Bros Ltd., the largest toy manufacturer in the world in the 1930s, whose trade names included Triang Toys. The firm was formed by George and Joseph Lines in the middle of the 19th century. By 1913 the company, then run only by Joseph, had five small factories in London. After the First World War three of Joseph's sons—Will, Arthur, and Walter—reformed the factory under the name Lines Bros Ltd., and soon set up new premises in Merton, Southwest London. The Pedigree name was registered in 1931, and by 1938 a whole variety of Pedigree Pets—toys on wheels—were being made under the Pedigree Soft Toys label. The toys were sold throughout the world and factories were set up in New Zealand, Canada, Australia, and South Africa. In 1946 they opened a factory in Belfast, Ireland, which took over the bulk of soft-toy production, making bears, both jointed and unjointed, primarily in mohair. Separate muzzles were introduced in the 1960s by the new designer, Ann Wood, who had previously worked at Deans, and new synthetic materials were used. Some bears had musical boxes, and a line of character toys was also produced. In 1971, Lines Bros ceased production and bear production transferred to Canterbury Bears. Pedigree's production manager, Jim Mulholland, set up his own factory called Mulholland and Bailie in Belfast, which is still producing teddy bears under the brand name of Nylena today.

RIGHT The fact that this Pedigree bear has a label saying he was made in England dates him to before 1955, when all soft-toy production moved to Ireland. He is very similar in style to the later examples in this section, with short limbs and no claw stitching on his velveteen paw pads. He has a black stitched nose and mouth and amber and black glass eyes. His gold mohair coat is still in excellent condition.
Height: 21in (53cm)
Approx value: $280

c.1850	G. and J. Lines Ltd. established by George and Joseph Lines
1919	Lines Brothers Limited established by William, Arthur, and Walter Lines
1924	Triang Toys registered. New factory set up in Merton, S.W. London
1931	Pedigree name registered
1946	Pedigree moves the bulk of its soft-toy production to Belfast, Ireland
	Pedigree set up in New Zealand
1947	Pedigree set up in Canada
1951	Pedigree set up in Australia
1960	Separate muzzles introduced on bears
1971	Lines Brothers ceases business and the name is taken over by Canterbury Bears

ABOVE Pedigree are wellknown for their dogs on wheels. This one has a label saying it was made in Northern Ireland. He is mohair and has a black plastic nose and tongue. It is unusual to find one in as good condition as this; most have been worn out with play.
Height: 17in (43cm)
Approx value: $80

ABOVE This 1960s golly is in perfect condition and has all his original features. His face, hands, and feet are cotton, his hair is synthetic, and he is stuffed with foam. The eyes, mouth, and jacket are all felt. He is smartly dressed in a yellow brocade vest and green corduroy pants.
Height: 23in (58cm)
Approx value: $280

ABOVE Pedigree bears often have the ears of this 1950s example, with the inner edges folded inward and sewn into the horizontal head seam. He is a typical Pedigree, with short chubby arms, pointed paws, straight legs, and no foot definition. His nose is felt, and his muzzle is pronounced.
Height: 20in (51cm)
Approx value: $320

ABOVE This 1950s gold mohair bear has black and amber plastic eyes and is fully jointed. He has a large round head and eyes set rather low on his face. His ears are very small in proportion to his head and are set at an angle. He has the Pedigree label sewn into his back seam.
Height: 17in (43cm)
Approx value: $280

ABOVE Short, straight legs with round paw pads and non-defined feet are common features of Pedigree bears. This 1950s cinnamon mohair example is very similar in shape to the one on the left, but he has particularly short stumpy arms and much larger, floppier ears than most Pedigrees.
Height: 14in (35.5cm)
Approx value: $160

ABOVE By the 1960s when this bear was made, the muzzle was separate from the rest of the head, but the "T"-shaped stitching of the mouth had not changed from earlier designs. He is mohair, but others at this time had synthetic fur. To compete with other novelty bears, he has bells in his ears.
Height: 15in (38cm)
Approx value: $160

Other English Makers

More and more British manufacturers are being discovered that produced bears during the first half of the 20th century. Although the major names are very well documented, many of the smaller firms made bears for a relatively short time and have now faded into obscurity. Some bears, such as those made by Steevans, are labeled, but there is still little known about the factory. Others, such as those made by Invicta, have only recently been rediscovered. Many English bears that appear for sale throughout the country are not labeled, but a little research can provide the purchaser with some answers. Particularly useful are old toy catalogs and ads, which not only bring to light new manufacturers but also illustrate the bears they produced. A little time exploring your bear's origins can be very rewarding.

HARWIN AND CO. LTD.

Harwin and Co. Ltd. was one of the first British manufacturers of teddy bears. They established their factory in 1914 at the Eagle Works in Finsbury Park, London, and produced a wide range of animals and dolls. They made their first bears in 1915, and at the London Fair in 1916 launched a series of mascot Ally Bears dressed in the uniforms of the allied forces of the First World War. The sales manager of the firm, Mr. Taylor, had previously been the traveling salesman for the German bear manufacturer, Steiff, and there are many similarities between the two's bears. However, whereas Steiff dressed few of their bears, Harwin dressed most of theirs. Although the Ally Bears continued to appear in ads up to the end of the First World War, the firm was soon affected by the postwar depression, and ceased trading in 1930.

RIGHT Harwin's Ally bears are very rare and collectible today. This particular example, known as Lord Kitchener, is dressed in the uniform of a First World War British officer. He is fully jointed, has black button eyes, gold mohair, and felt paw pads with stitched claws. He is in perfect condition and his original clothes are all intact. The best way to identify Harwin bears is to study old ads.
Height: 12in (30.5cm)
Approx value: $8,300 plus

RIGHT This Steevans bear from around 1918 is made of rose pink mohair, which has faded considerably. He can be identified by the metal tag in his right ear. He has horizontal nose stitching and three black-stitched claws on his paws and feet.
Height: 12in (30.5cm)
Approx value: $1,200–1,800

STEEVANS MANUFACTURING CO.

Very little is known about this English toy factory apart from the fact that it was founded around 1908 and ceased production in 1920. Some ads show that Steevans produced a number of bears with musical chimes inside the body. The bears were originally labeled with a metal button in the ear with the words "Steevans, England" and a serial number embossed on it, and this makes it possible to identify several of them today. A number of similar examples have been discovered without a label, but when compared with documented ones, it seems likely they were also made by Steevans (*see p.81*). Because Steevans produced bears for a relatively short time, few survive today, and their high quality and endearing faces make them particularly sought-after. They share the characteristics of many early British bears, with black boot-button eyes and hard stuffing.

LEFT This bear is typical of those produced by Chad Valley under the Peacock label. Made around 1932, this example is in excellent condition and still has the red and white printed Peacock label on his right foot pad.
Height: 28in (71cm)
Approx value: $3,000

PEACOCK AND SONS

Peacock and Sons was established in London in 1853 as makers of toys and games. They registered as William Peacock and Co. in 1908, and in 1918 changed their name to Peacock and Co. Ltd. Chad Valley bought the company in 1931 and produced a line of bears with the Peacock label from its factory in Clerkenwell, East London. These bears have black horizontally stitched noses that are very similar in style to those on Chad Valley's Magna bear (*see p.65*). Other features in common with Chad bears include:
•large cupped ears
•four stitched claws on foot pads
•large chest
•long arms
•"drumstick" legs
The Peacock label was not used after 1940.

RIGHT This Invicta bear from around 1948 has many of the characteristics of Farnell bears, including a bright gold luxurious coat, large ears, and an unshaven muzzle. He has brown and black glass eyes and brown vertical nose stitching similar to that of Farnell bears of the time.
Height: 28in (71cm)
Approx value: $850

INVICTA TOYS LTD

Invicta Toys was founded in 1935 by two former employers of J. K. Farnell—Mr. G. E. Beer and Mr. T. B. Wright. From their factory at Park Royal Road in North West London they made a large range of toys, including animals on wheels, bears, cats, dogs, monkeys, and many other creatures. During the Second World War the factory virtually ceased production of bears to manufacture armaments. However, after the War the firm took on more workers and the business prospered. Many of the firm's bears were produced for export. Mr. Beer retired in 1954 and the firm closed down. In the past many Invicta bears have been wrongly identified as Farnell bears, because of the many similarities between the two's designs. However, new evidence has come to light recently, including a number of photographs of positively identified Invicta bears, which suggests that some of the bears previously identified as Farnell could actually have been made by Invicta instead.

NORAH WELLINGS

Norah Wellings started in business in 1926, producing cloth dolls in partnership with her brother Leonard from her factory in Wellington, Shropshire, and it is these dolls that she is best known for today. She had previously been a designer at Chad Valley and it is probably her experience there that led her to produce a number of teddy bears. She did not make them in the traditional way, but simply adapted the patterns she had used for her dolls. Consequently, most of them have cloth bodies, and are dressed in brightly-colored cotton clothes. She also produced a number of mascots and novelty items. She continued to produce bears and dolls after the Second World War, but retired after her brother died in 1960. Her dolls and bears are usually well labeled with a paper swing-tag with the words "Norah Wellings Productions," and also a sewn-in embroidered label.

LEFT This Norah Wellings bear dates from the 1950s. He is wearing the typical printed cotton dungarees of many of her bears. Others had material balloon-shaped legs. This example is in mint condition and still has its original label.
Height: 15in (38cm)
Approx value: $950

PIXIE TOYS

Pixie Toys was founded in the 1930s by the wives of two glass manufacturers who had a works near Stourbridge. They were undergoing hard times and the two women decided to set up a soft toy company to generate some extra income. Their first bears were made at home, but soon the women relocated the business to their husbands' glassworks. They employed a designer, Mrs. Elizabeth Simmonds, who had once worked for Merrythought and for Norah Wellings (*see above*). The influence of Mrs. Simmonds' time at Merrythought can be seen in the design of their bears, particularly in the distinctive webbed claw stitching (*see the bear on the right*). When the family retired at the end of the 1930s Elizabeth Simmonds bought out Pixie Toys with a business partner, Major Brittle. The company went into decline for a while, before being taken over again around 1955 and finally closing down in 1962.

RIGHT This bear was made in the 1950s. He has golden mohair and has a square-shaped stitched nose with long dropped ends. He is in very good condition and still has the original Pixie label on his foot.
Height: 15in (38cm)
Approx value: $600

LEFRAY TOYS LTD.

Lefray was established in London in 1948. In 1960 they relocated to St. Albans in Hertfordshire, where they traded for nine years before moving to their current location in South Wales. The factory took over another British manufacturer, Real Soft Toys, in 1980, producing that firm's toys under a separate label. Lefray was granted the license to produce a soft toy version of Rupert Bear, which they continue to produce today. Lefray bears display many typical English characteristics, including short limbs, high quality golden mohair, and large floppy ears. The bear shown here is a typical example. He is very similar in style to a number of unlabeled synthetic plush examples produced in the 1950s and 1960s (*see p.81*).

LEFT This typical Lefray bear from the 1950s has a golden mohair coat, brown cloth pads, and orange and black plastic eyes. The growler mechanism inside his chest is operated by pulling a cord in his back. He is in very good condition and still has the original label on his foot.
Height: 38in (69cm)
Approx value: $150–300

RIGHT Tinka Bell was based upon the fairy in J. M. Barrie's stories of Peter Pan. The bear was extremely popular in the 1950s, with thousands being produced each week during a busy period. She was made in a variety of different versions and sizes.
Height: 18in (46cm)
Approx value: $300

PLUMMER WANDLESS & CO.

Plummer Wandless & Co. was formed by Daphne Plummer and her husband John, after Daphne had dismantled a toy rabbit she bought in Sussex in 1944 to see how it was made. Inspired to make her own toys, she began making bears for some extra money with quite a lot of success. When her husband came out of the army after the War, he saw the potential in bears and gave up his job in the furniture trade to make them. His friend Dudley Wandless pooled his money with John, and together they set up business in 1946. Within ten years they were producing around 24 different designs. The bears were made from John's designs, using pastel-dyed sheepskin with a silky gloss. The first toys were hand-stitched, but the factory soon used machines. By 1967 they were producing around 70,000 teddy bears. Unfortunately, Daphne died in 1971 and the business was sold, but her bears live on.

WENDY BOSTON

Wendy and Ken Boston set up their soft toy manufacturing business in 1945 in South Wales. They pioneered the safety screw-in locked plastic eyes, and in 1954 they revolutionized bear manufacturing when they introduced the first washable bear to Britain. The company was taken over by Denys Fisher Toys in 1968 and finally ceased production in 1976. Because Wendy Boston concentrated on bears that were easy to wash and durable, she often used synthetic fabrics such as nylon, and filled the bears with a rubber foam. However, she did also produce a line of mohair bears. Most of her bears are unjointed with undefined feet, and often have ears in one piece with the head (apparently so they could be hung on a clothes line without the ears falling off!). They come in a range of colors and in short and long pile plush. The label includes instructions to wash in "luke-warm suds."

RIGHT These two synthetic plush Wendy Boston bears from 1958 are typical. Because her bears are unjointed, most were made in the perma-nent sitting position seen here.
Height: 15in (38cm) each
Approx value: $120 each

RIGHT Two unidenti-fied bears from the early 20th century. Typical characteristics include:
•black button eyes
•musical chimes
•no paw pads
•cotton foot pads
•short mohair
•hard stuffing
•large ears

IDENTIFYING ENGLISH BEARS

As many English bears have no labels, the only way to identify them is to compare them with similar examples that are docu-mented. By comparing the characteristics of the two bears on the left with each other and with the Steevans bear on p.79, it seems almost certain that these two were made by the same manufacturer, probably Steevans. The pink bear on the right is typical of the lower-quality English bears produced after the Second World War by many different factories. Characteristics include short artificial plush, large floppy ears, amber and black plastic eyes, short limbs, and rounded feet.

Irish Makers

Gaeltarra Eireann literally means "goods of the Irish-speaking part of Ireland" and is the name of a government board set up in 1938 as part of Gaeltacht Services Division which attempted to foster and develop local handicraft industries. The Division set up three factories to manufacture toys and small utility goods, each with its own manager, subsidised by the State, and with all administration and distribution carried out by civil servants. The bears and soft toys were made at Elly Bay, Co. Mayo under the name of Erris Toys until 1953, when the name then changed to Tara Toys. The Gaeltarra Eireann took over the running of the industries from the civil service in 1958, and the soft toy industry was moved from Elly Bay to Crolly, Co. Donegal in 1969, where it continued to produce toys under the new name of Soltoys Ltd., until 1979. The early bears were made of mohair and natural pile fabrics imported from Britain and the Continent, and were hand-stuffed with cotton flock and wood-wool, but in later years synthetic fabrics were used. Earlier bears were jointed, but later ones had fixed limbs. From around 1958 plastic eyes and noses were introduced.

ABOVE This bear was made around 1947. He has a cotton plush body and stubby feet with felt plush paw pads. He is fully jointed and has a squeaker in his lower body. The wording on the label—*Brégáin Iorruis Déantüs na Gaeltachta*—translates as "Erris Toys, made in the Gaeltacht."
Height: 12½in (32 cm)
Approx value: $160

RIGHT The unique nose stitching on this bear means that although he has no label he can be identified as a later Tara Toys bear. His paws would originally have been rexine, but are now felt. The tapering arms and slightly curved paws are very similar to those on the earlier Erris bears.
Height: 22½in (56cm)
Approx value: $300

1937-49	Eire used on labels, rather than Made in Ireland.
1938	Gaeltarra Eireann starts producing teddy bears under the name of Erris Toys.
1950-65	Hans Weberpals, former Sonneberg designer, is Production Manager at Gaeltarra Eireann.
1953	Gaeltarra Eireann starts making bears under the name of Tara Toys.
1958	Gaeltarra Eireann takes over the running of the toy industry from the civil service.
1965	Hans Weberpals sets up Celtic Toys.
1969	Gealtarra Eireann moves to County Donegal, making bears under the name of Soltoys.
1979	Soltoys ceases production.

ABOVE LEFT AND RIGHT "Timothy" was made by Tara Toys in the early 1950s, and has a label sewn in his foot saying "Made in the Republic of Ireland." He has a mohair body and rexine pads, and his eyes are made from plastic. A novelty design, he has a mouth that opens by using a lever attached to the back of his head (*see picture*). He has the unusual downturned stitching on his nose which is a characteristic of bears made by Tara Toys.
Height: 16in (41cm)
Approx value: $450

BELOW RIGHT These two later bears from the 1960s are typical of the less expensive Gaeltarra Eireann range. They are made of bri-nylon, including their paws, and have plastic eyes and noses. Like many later Irish bears, the small bear is not jointed. He has an open mouth and a red felt tongue. The larger bear is fully jointed, and has an unusual upturned nose which, with his large eyes, gives him a sad expression.
Height: *left* 11$\frac{1}{2}$in (29cm); *right* 23$\frac{1}{2}$in (60cm)
Approx value: $175 each

Two 1970s Celtic bears.
Height: 12in (33cm) each
Approx value: $150 each

CELTIC TOYS
In 1965 Hans Weberpals left Gaeltarra Eireann and together with a partner set up his own factory called Celtic Toys, in Millstreet, Co. Cork. He produced teddy bears, but in order to keep his business thriving he also made other products, including anoraks! The company closed down in 1975, but was revived in 1978, concentrating on children's clothing. Their only toys were made for promotional purposes, but they still bear the Celtic Toys label. Both the Celtic bears shown here were made in the early 1970s, and they show distinct similarities to the bears of the Tara Toys period. They are made entirely from synthetic fabrics, including their eyes and noses, which typically at this time are plastic. The bears are unjointed and have been fixed in a rather uncomfortable looking semi-sitting position. Typical Irish characteristics include short limbs, dual-color bodies, and wide-apart ears. Although it is not visible in the photograph, the black and white bear on the far left has the addition of a small black tail.

French Bears

France was already famous for its mechanical toys when at the turn of the 20th century, toy manufacturer Fernand Martin made the first toy bear—a ferocious looking bear that shuffled along on metal feet. However, it was not until around 1919 that the first mohair bear was produced, by Marcel Pintel, with Fadap soon following suit. Bears produced in France between 1925 and 1940 tend to look rather similar, probably because designers often changed firms and took their designs with them. They are usually of short bristle mohair, and often have simple jointing visible on the outside of the body. With the Second World War most toy manufacturers understandably ceased activities, but in the 1950s the industry revived, and over 25 known firms were active. Unfortunately, this burst of acitvity was short-lived. The 1960s saw the decline of the traditional bear, and its replacement with less expensive, one-piece, washable bears. Today only one firm, Blanchet, still produces traditional bears. Early French bears are rare, particularly outside of France, and many of those found are not labeled.

LEFT Three 1930s French bears sitting in their dressing room.

RIGHT A lovely 1930s Fadap bear, dressed in his French beret.

M. Pintel Fils

M. Pintel Fils was the earliest manufacturer of plush teddy bears in France. Marcel Pintel began making stuffed toys (*les jouets bourrés*) for his father's firm in Paris in 1913. He was full of enthusiasm and ideas, and wanted his toys to compete with imported ones. The first Pintel bear, a mechanical tumbling clown, appeared in their 1911 catalog, and in 1913 their trademark featuring two embracing bears was registered. Production slowed during the First World War, but by 1919 Marcel had developed a new line of stuffed dolls and animals. The first mohair bears, produced a year later, were very delicate, firmly filled, and had tapering limbs. They were so popular that part of Pintel's bear production had to be sent out to other toy makers such as Thiennot (*see p.92*). During the Second World War the firm had to close down, but production started up again after the War using whatever materials were available. Bears continued to be produced under the Pintel name until 1976, when business ceased altogether. Early Pintel bears, up until the 1930s, have a metal identification button attached to their chest.

ABOVE These two bears are among the earliest examples made by Pintel. They have glass eyes and are fully jointed. The cinnamon bear on the right retains its original paw pads with three claws.
Height: 15in (38cm) each
Approx value: $450-750 each

RIGHT This is typical of Pintel's earliest mohair bears. Made around 1920, he has the original Pintel button attached to his chest. He has the characteristic nose stitching and large feet.
Height: 15in (38cm)
Approx value: $2,300

ABOVE The early French toy tradition centered around mechanical toys, so it is not surprising that the country's first teddy bears were mechanical. This bear on a tricycle was one of the very earliest bears produced by Pintel and was made around 1915. It was a very popular design and continued in production until 1940. The body of the bear is made of metal, and is covered in felt, and the eyes are glass. His nose and mouth are now missing.
Height: 8in (20cm)
Approx value: $850

LEFT Between 1927 and 1930 Pintel produced a number of bears that were mounted on wheels. Although this example is not marked, comparisons with a similar Pintel bear featured in a 1927 ad for a Paris department store suggest that this one was also made by them. The body is of felt, rather than the metal of earlier examples, and is firmly stuffed with wood wool. He has boot-button eyes and a horizontally stitched nose. He is standing on a painted metal frame with wooden wheels, and has a particularly nice shape.
Height: 9in (23cm) including frame
Approx value: $750

BELOW The long, tapering arms, big feet, serious expression, and firm wood wool stuffing all suggest that this unmarked bear from around 1925 was made by Pintel. He is in very good condition and still has original nose- and mouth-stitching.
Height: 15in (38cm)
Approx value: $750

LEFT The large Pintel bear on the left, made around 1925, has characteristically large feet. The bear on the right, from the 1950s, was made by I.C.O. Typically, his ears are lined with a lighter color mohair than the rest of his body.
Height: *left* 19in (48cm); *right* 13in (33cm)
Approx value: *left*; $600
right $230

DISTINGUISHING CHARACTERISTICS OF EARLY PINTEL BEARS (TO c.1930)

• tapering arms

• eyes stitched into the back of the head

• long, large feet

• long muzzle

• vertical nose stitching with a longer stitch at either end

• cotton paw pads with three claws

• long limbs

• voice box

LEFT This lovely cinnamon bear from the late 1920s is almost identical to earlier examples, but his nose does not have the downturned stitches of many others. He also looks a little happier than many Pintel bears. His glass eyes have retained their amber and black color— in many other cases the eyes have worn clear.
Height: 19in (48.4cm)
Approx value: $2,300

Pintel's trademark button featuring two embracing bears was regis- tered in 1913, and was used to identify their bears until the 1930s.

1920s nose, show-
ing vertical stitch-
ing and long ends

1930s nose on
bears with shaved
inset muzzles

1950s noses were
almost identical to
earlier ones

RIGHT This Shirley Temple
doll with lovely blond curls
is believed to be by Pintel.
She is made of felt, is rod-
jointed, and is still wearing all
her original clothes. Pictured
with her is an unknown 1930s
French bear, and a small synthetic bear with a plastic nose,
which was made by J.P.M.
Height: *doll* 16in (40cm),
large bear 17in (43cm),
small bear 6in (15cm)
Approx value: *doll* $380;
large bear $230 *small bear* $75

ABOVE Around 1925 Pintel
employed a new designer who
developed a new style of bear,
with a set-in muzzle of clipped
mohair, a larger head, eyes and
ears, and a small body. These
two bears from around 1937
are typical. They are stuffed
with kapok rather than wood
wool, which gives them a
softer body than earlier bears.
Height: *left* 22in (56cm);
right 15in (38cm)
Approx value: $530 each

ABOVE Bears from 1938 to
1940 were made from whatever
materials were available. This
example has a woolen blanket
body and red velvet ears.
Height: 15in (38cm)
Approx value: $230

ABOVE Later bears, such as
this one from the late 1940s,
had clipped mohair plush. He
is firmly stuffed with wood
wool, although others at this
time were stuffed with kapok,
which was introduced into
France in the 1930s.
Height: 20in (50cm)
Approx value: $530

Fadap

Fadap (*Fabrication Artistique d'Animaux en Peluche*) started to make bears from its factory in Divonne-les-Bains in France in 1925. The early bears are tubby, with large, pear-shaped bodies, long arms, and thick paws. They are quite similar to those made by Pintel, but one way of differentiating between the two is that Fadap bears tend to have more upturned noses than those made by Pintel. They also often have a seam underneath the chin. Identifying characteristics of Fadap's early bears are their black button eyes, four claws, and voice box. They were often stuffed with wood wool, but feel softer than many Pintel bears. A metal button with the words "Fadap" and "France" embossed on it was fixed to one ear with a paper tag attached to it, but this is very often missing. During the Second World War Fadap slowed production but it did not close down until 1978.

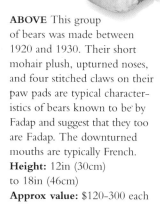

ABOVE This group of bears was made between 1920 and 1930. Their short mohair plush, upturned noses, and four stitched claws on their paw pads are typical characteristics of bears known to be by Fadap and suggest that they too are Fadap. The downturned mouths are typically French.
Height: 12in (30cm) to 18in (46cm)
Approx value: $120–300 each

RIGHT Because French bears are all so similar it is particularly difficult to identify them if they have lost their labels. This lovely bear from the 1930s has many typical characteristics of Fadap bears, but he does not have the metal tag in his ear so it is not possible to attribute him with certainty to Fadap.
Height: 16in (40.5cm)
Approx value: $230

Engraved metal ear button
introduced c.1928

Paper label used with
metal ear button above

ABOVE Believed to
have been made around 1928,
this wonderful bear has all the
typical characteristics of Fadap,
and the fact that he still has
his button in his ear will
add to his collectibility.
Height: 18in (46cm)
Approx value: $980

ABOVE It is unusual to find
bears such as this one, which
still has his original paper label
in his ear. Dating from around
1938, he has clear glass eyes
and a tilt growler, which
is still in working order.
Height: 24in (61cm)
Approx value: $830

ABOVE Design changed little
after the Second World War,
and this bear from the 1940s
shares many of the typical
characteristics of Fadap's
earlier bears. His short mohair
coat is in perfect condition.
Height: 19in (48cm)
Approx value: $600

LEFT Most Fadap bears made
before the Second World War
had cotton paw pads. Those on
this bear, probably made by
Fadap in the 1930s, are a little
frayed in places.
Height: 15in (38cm)
Approx value: $680

LEFT The bear standing
behind his brood is believed
to have been made by Fadap
in the 1930s. He is in a rather
sorry state with his threadbare
coat, and has an unusually
large downturned mouth.
Apart from the black bear,
which was made by Blanchet
in the 1960s, the multi-colored
group surrounding him are of
unknown origin. Thought to
have been made in the 1930s,
they are *fétiche* bears—mascots
carried by the French in their
pockets for good luck. Typical
French characteristics include:
•differently colored ear lining
from the rest of the body
•narrow, horizontally stitched
nose with downturned ends
•black boot-button eyes
•visible metal joints
•short mohair plush
•visible metal rod joints
Height: *Fadap* 8in (20cm);
fétiche bears 4in (10cm)
Approx value: *Fadap* $230;
fétiche bears $75-120 each

Other French Makers

In addition to Pintel and Fadap, a number of other manufacturers also produced bears before the Second World War, including Thiennot, Faye, and Alfa Paris. Unfortunately, the War put a stop to most teddy bear production for almost ten years, but the 1950s saw a revival. Over 25 makers were listed at the 1951 Toy Fair (*Salon du Jouet*) in France, and it is possible that even more manufacturers were in operation at this time. The ads from the catalog of this fair are very useful in helping to identify many bears, although they provide little factual information about the companies. Most of these 1950s bears seem to be of mohair, and are fully jointed. Those featured here are typical examples. Pintel and Fadap were also still making bears throughout this period.

EMILE THIENNOT

Emile Thiennot initially worked for Marcel Pintel, but in 1919 he set up his own toy manufacturing company in Piney, selling bears and other stuffed animals under the trade name of Le Jouet Champenois. In 1920 he won a medal for one of his teddy bears at a competition in France. The firm changed its trade name to Création Tieno in 1957, and closed down in January 1993. Later bears are mainly of synthetic plush materials and were designed for young babies. Thiennot also made replicas of their early designs (*see p. 120*). The early bears are difficult to identify because they are not labeled, and many could be mistaken for those made by Pintel, reflecting the influence of Thiennot's time there.

RIGHT The large 1930s bear is made of white flannel and has red cotton pads—the material inside his ears is also red. The bear displays the very basic jointing used on many French bears. Typically, the head is unjointed, and the body is barrel-shaped. The horizontal nose stitching and very sad mouth are characteristically French. The little blue bear was made by Faye, manufacturers of bears in the 1930s. He has metal rods for his arms and legs, white cotton paw pads, and no lining to his ears. Typically, his head is unjointed. **Height:** *right* 27in (68.5cm); *left* 12in (30.5cm) **Approx value:** *left* $230; *right* $380

Two cotton Alfa Paris bears from the 1950s.

Height: 13in (33cm) each
Approx value: $150 each

ALFA PARIS

Alfa (*Article de Luxe Fabrication Artisanale*) was founded in Paris in 1934 and produced its first bear in 1936. The excellent quality and original designs of their bears made them successful for over 40 years. Alfa Paris bears always have a big smile; most are dressed, even wearing underwear and shoes. They are easy to identify because they have "Alfa" printed underneath the right foot. Alfa Paris are best known for their unjointed bears dressed as little boys or girls. Only the visible parts are mohair; the body and arms are made of fabric. Their clothes are usually made of gingham or dotted material, and shoes are often matching. Designs varied little, but after the Second World War synthetic materials replaced mohair, and glass eyes were replaced by plastic. Other animals were made in a similar design, including rabbits and chickens. After the War, Alfa Paris also made jointed bears.

1950s Jan Jac bear

1950 O'Lis bear

JAN JAC

The Paris-based manufacturer, Jan Jac, is one of the many French companies who produced bears in the 1950s. A common feature on these later bears is a red felt tongue, seen on this example—the long, shaggy mohair is also typical. This bear has short arms and a square face, and is quite different from those by Pintel and Fadap.
Height: 20in (51cm)
Approx value: $270

O'LIS

O'Lis, a toy-manufacturer based in Saint-Étienne, also produced bears in the 1950s. The example on the left, made under license to Walt Disney as Winnie the Pooh, has large movable googly eyes set very close together.
Height: 19in (48cm)
Approx value: $300

1950s BEARS

Many of the manufacturers producing bears in the 1950s have no documentation, and it is only through their labels and advertising that we know they were even producing bears. Shown here is a hug of typical French bears from the 1950s. They were made, from left to right, by Marjo (*Manufactuer Rémoise de Jouet*) of Reims, Ragonneau of Paris, Blanchet of Pont St. Esprit, and Sidaf of St. Etienne. Out of all of these manufacturers, only Blanchet is still making bears today.

Typical French characteristics include:
•large cupped ears
•distinctive downturned mouth
•cotton plush fabric
•fabric nose
•hard-stuffed body
•short limbs
•cotton paw pads

American Bears

President Theodore "Teddy" Roosevelt is credited as the inspiration behind the first teddy bear *(see p. 14)*, so it is not surprising that bears were the passion of thousands of Americans in the early years of the 20th century (to such an extent that they became known as the teddy bear years!). Morris Michtom's Ideal Novelty and Toy Company (allegedly manufacturers of the first teddy bear), dominated production, but other important makers included Knickerbocker, Bruin, Aetna, Gund—who still make bears today—and the Character Toy Company. Novelty teddy bears, which could growl, squeak, laugh, whistle, and even tumble, were made from around 1910.

American bears are very popular with collectors, especially anything by Ideal. Early examples are very rare and are much in demand. Not all American makers marked their bears, but many American bears have distinguishing characteristics, such as a long firm body and short, straight limbs.

LEFT Both these bears were made around 1907, the one standing, by Aetna, and the one seated, by Bruin.

RIGHT The two standing bears in this group were made by Knickerbocker, the large one in the 1930s, and the small one in the 1950s. The sitting bear was made by Ideal around 1906.

The Ideal Novelty and Toy Co.

The Ideal Novelty and Toy Company was set up in New York in 1903 by Rose and Morris Michtom, the couple reputed to have produced the very first teddy bear, based on the now-famous Clifford Berryman cartoon showing President Roosevelt's encounter with a bear (*see p.12*). Initially Ideal made only teddy bears, but their line soon expanded to include character dolls and animals. They moved to larger premises in Brownsville, Brooklyn, in 1907, and had headquarters in Newark, New Jersey. Designs changed little up until the beginning of the Second World War. However, when Morris died in 1938, the company was taken over by his son, Benjamin, and new designs and materials were introduced and the name was altered to Ideal Toy Corporation. The company also started to label its bears with a stitched label and a paper tag in the shape of a circus wagon.

Early Ideal bears do not appear to have been labeled, making positive identification difficult. However, certain characteristics are typical to their bears. Comparing bears not known to be Ideal with Ideal bears that have remained with the same family since they were purchased at the beginning of the century may also help to identify some of these early bears as Ideal. Very early Ideal bears are similar to those made by Steiff (*see pp.22-33*).

RIGHT Despite this bear's rather battered appearance, he still has the lovely appealing face of many Ideal bears. Made around 1905, he is absolutely typical of their designs from this early period. Identifying characteristics of early Ideal bears include:
•wide triangular head that is flat at the back
•short mohair
•large, round ears set on the side of the head
•pads on the feet that taper to a definite point
•long and slender body
•long muzzle
•arms set low on the body
•excelsior stuffing
Height: 13in (33cm)
Approx value: $900–1,000

BELOW These two old Ideal soldiers from around 1907 and 1910 are dressed in their original Teddy Roosevelt Rough Rider outifts— however, their shoes and medals are more recent additions. Only those parts of the body that are visible outside of their clothing are mohair— the rest of the body is made of plain cotton, in a design similar to the dressed Bingie bears made by the British manufacturer, Merrythought (*see p. 68*). Both these bears are stuffed with excelsior. The seated bear has shoe-button eyes; the one standing has glass.
Height: *left* 20in (51cm); *right* 15$\frac{1}{2}$in (40cm)
Approx value: $1,800

ABOVE This is possibly one of the earliest bears attributed to the Ideal Toy Company. He is unusual because he has leather paw pads and a felt nose, which may both be features of the very first bears the firm produced.
Height: 14in (35.6cm)
Approx value: $750-900

ABOVE This is one of the famous googly-eyed Ideal bears reputedly thrown from the back of a train by Teddy Roosevelt during his election campaign in 1904, and thought to be based on Clifford Berryman's cartoon bear (*see p. 12*).
Height: 11in (28cm)
Approx value: $1,500

ABOVE The large, horizontally stitched nose and triangular face of this blond mohair bear suggest he was made by Ideal. This shaved muzzle is unusually long. Other blond Ideal bears have brown stitching.
Height: 12$\frac{1}{2}$in (32cm)
Approx value: $1,800 plus

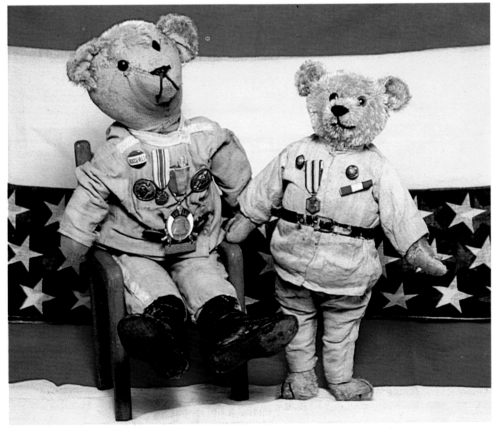

ABOVE The sitting position of this bear, made in 1905, shows the characteristic foot pads of early Ideal bears, which have very rounded heels tapering to sharp points at the toes. This bear has his claws sewn onto the pads, but others do not. The muzzle is less pointed than on earlier bears, and the profile of the head shows similarities with the bears made by Hecla (*see p. 101*).
Height: 13in (33cm)
Approx value: $1,500

The earliest bears have a long sloping muzzle and a large, felt nose.

c.1904 googly-eyed bear has a shaved, shorter muzzle.

c.1905 bear with charac-teristic long, shaved muzzle.

c.1905 alternative design with a profile similar to that of Hecla bears.

c.1909 bear with head set deep into the body, and ears far back.

BELOW The quality of workmanship on this bear from around 1909 is a bit uneven—one of his foot pads is much larger than the other! However, he is in excellent condition for his age and is made of very high quality mohair. Early Ideal bears had either horizon-tally stitched noses or the type featured on this example, made from a piece of twill fabric and sewn onto the muzzle.
Height: 18in (46cm)
Approx value: $1,700 plus

ABOVE This Ideal bear is wearing a pair of overalls with letters "Teddy B" embroidered on the front. Others had the name "Teddy G". These were the names of the Roosevelt bears created by American author Seymour Eaton, who wrote many books about the bears (*see pp.150-1*). His stories were so popular they inspired a whole line of merchandise featuring the bears. Modern reproductions have been made in recent years by D & D Productions of Maryland.
Height: 10in (25.4cm)
Approx value: *bear* $875; *overalls* $100

ABOVE Like a number of bears made by Ideal, this exam-ple, from around 1907, shares many characteristics with Steiff bears, including very long limbs and large narrow feet. Although the earliest Ideal bears were stuffed with wood wool, this example is stuffed with excel-sior, which makes him softer to touch. His mohair coat is very short, and looks almost like wool. His particularly large nose, triangular in shape, is made of woven floss, and he has black shoe-button eyes. Early Ideal bears with large eyes have boot- rather than shoe-buttons.
Height: 17in (43cm)
Approx value: $1,800

c.1919 bear sticking out his red felt tongue. He has smaller ears.

1920 bear with a shorter muzzle and ears set on top of the head.

1950s Smokey-type bear with painted features on vinyl face.

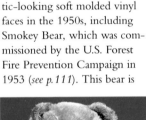

BELOW After the First World War Ideal, like most other American toy manufacturers, used glass eyes instead of black buttons. The body shape has changed significantly by this time, too, and is now quite round—this example has a somewhat football-shaped body. By this time the bears no longer have humps on their backs, and their limbs are much shorter, with small feet and less pointed paw pads.
Height: 23in (58.5cm)
Approx value: $1,000

ABOVE RIGHT Ideal made a number of bears with realistic-looking soft molded vinyl faces in the 1950s, including Smokey Bear, which was commissioned by the U.S. Forest Fire Prevention Campaign in 1953 (*see p.111*). This bear is very similar in style to Smokey Bear. He has airbrushed features on his face, but other examples had moving glass eyes. Some of the bears had plastic molded hands and feet.
Height: 12in (30.5cm)
Approx value: $65

ABOVE The remains of a red felt tongue make this Ideal bear from around 1919 particularly unusual. His ears are smaller than earlier examples, but they are still positioned on the side of the head. His nose is also different—stitched vertically over a piece of black fabric. Boot button eyes were not used on their bears after the First World War.
Height: 12in (30.5cm)
Approx value: $1,500

ABOVE Special editions were popular with American manufacturers in the 1970s. Ideal made this bear in 1978 for their 75th anniversary. Made of synthetic plush, he has little in common with early Ideal bears. He comes in a special box that is also highly collectible and that will add considerably to the value in the future.
Height: 16in (40.5cm)
Approx value: $125

Other Early U.S. Makers

Teddy bear fever reached a peak in the United States between 1906 and 1907, following President Roosevelt's re-election. A great number of manufacturers started to make teddy bears, producing traditional designs as well as a vast array of novelties, such as the "Electric Eye" bears and the Laughing Roosevelt bear. The more traditional designs are of high quality; many closely resemble Steiffs, and often have a similar distinctive hump and realistically long arms. However, there were also many mass-produced bears, most of which cannot be attributed to a maker today. Among the most collectible of these early manufacturers are Bruin, Aetna, and Hecla. Many of these companies were only in business for a very short time, so the bears are quite rare.

THE LAUGHING ROOSEVELT BEAR

The New York-based Columbia Teddy Bear Manufacturers produced a number of jointed bears, but are best known for the Laughing Roosevelt Bear, made in 1907. This popular bear was designed to reproduce President Roosevelt's toothy grin! An advertisement in the 1907 edition of *Playthings* toy magazine states: "The Laughing Teddy Bear laughs and shows his teeth at critics. But the latest output of this well-known house has no critics to laugh at, and still he laughs. He is the newest and best stuffed animal toy on the market." The bear was made in different styles, but because only a limited number were produced, he is highly collectible today.

ABOVE This Laughing Roosevelt Bear was made in 1908. He has short, gold mohair, glass eyes, jointed arms and legs, and a swivel head. When the bear's tummy is squeezed, his mouth opens to reveal two white glass teeth set in a wooden jaw.
Height: 21in (54 cm)
Approx value: $3,500

RIGHT This old fellow is one of the earliest examples of a Laughing Roosevelt bear, and dates from around 1907. He is known as a Laughing Burlap Bear, because his body is made of brown nettle cloth fabric. This fierce-looking example has wooden teeth and jaws, whereas later bears have glass teeth. He is fully jointed and has the black boot-button eyes of most early bears. The bears have long bodies with very short arms.
Height: 14in (35.5cm)
Approx value $3,500

1907 Harman
Height: 18in
(35.5.cm)
**Approx
value:**
$530

Early Aetna
Height: 14in
(35.5.cm)
Approx value:
$3,000

HARMAN MANUFACTURING COMPANY

This New York company made a variety of teddy bears and bear-related items including a teddy bear purse, teddy dolls, and possums. They made animals with voice boxes, including nine different sizes of bears. These are not marked and are very rare today. The bear on the left has many typical characteristics, including short bristle mohair, arms set low on the body, and straight legs.

THE AETNA TOY ANIMAL COMPANY

The Aetna Toy Animal Company produced bears from around 1907, that were sold exclusively by the wholesaler George Borgfeldt and Co. in New York. Advertised as "The Aetna Bear (formerly the Keystone Bear)," the bears were of very high quality and of only top grade materials. An oval outline with the word "Aetna" was stamped on the base of the foot of each bear.

LEFT This Hecla bear from around 1907 has his head set characteristically deep into his body. Made of mohair, he is stuffed with excelsior and has clear glass eyes with painted backs.
Height: 14in (35.5.cm)
Approx value: $3,200

HECLA

Another short-lived American manufacturer from the early 1900s was Hecla, who made bears with voice boxes in direct competition to Steiff, importing mohair from Germany. Many of the bears were assembled by workers from German toy factories, and as a result it is very difficult to differentiate between those by Hecla and those by Steiff. Perhaps the most distinguishing characteristic is the ears, which on Hecla bears are set wide apart in typical American style. Hecla bears are very rare and sought after, and their high quality is evident in the example shown here. Other distinguishing characteristics of Hecla bears include the distinctive rust-colored nose and claw stitching and closely set eyes, made of clear glass and with painted backs. Similarities to Steiff bears include the hump on the bear's back, large round feet, and long limbs. The arms are set very high on the body, a feature of the bear pictured here.

Height: 14in
(35.5.cm) each
Approx value:
$3,000 plus each

BRUIN MANUFACTURING COMPANY (B.M.C.)

The New York-based Bruin Manfacturing Company produced bears for only a very short time between 1907 and 1909, and consequently they are very rare. They are some of the few American bears made in the early 1900s that still retain their labels —sewn on the sole of the foot with the letters "B.M.C." woven in gold. Their bears are very finely made. Typical characteristics include ears set onto the side of the head, a long pointed nose, and black shoe-button eyes placed close together. The two bears shown here are in excellent condition, and have the lovely silky mohair associated with B.M.C. B.M.C.'s blond bears have the characteristic light-brown nose and claw stitching seen on this example. The downturned paws on both these bears are a typical feature. They are fully jointed and stuffed with kapok to give them a soft body. It is these bears' particularly endearing expressions that make them so appealing to collectors. Many of them are actually smiling.

SELF-WHISTLING TEDDY BEAR

The Strauss Manufacturing Company, based in New York, produced toys, games, and bears at the beginning of the 20th century, including a number of novelties. They are particularly famous for their "self-whistling" bear, illustrated here, which was first advertised in the 1907 edition of *Playthings* magazine in the United States. Encased in the bear's body is a hollow tube with a movable weight that produces a whistling sound when the bear is turned upside down and back again. These bears are very rare today. The company also produced a musical bear that played music when a crank at the back was turned. The "self-whistling" bear shown here has the characteristic red cotton nose and claws, pointed muzzle, and long Steiff-like arms of these bears. However, his original leather paw pads have been replaced with cotton and his clothes are a recent addition.

LEFT A typical Strauss "self-whistling" bear from around 1907 with a modern whistle hung around his neck.
Height: 21in (53cm)
Approx value: $1,800

TOPSY-TURVY DOLL

The Albert Bruckner Company, founded in Jersey City, New Jersey, in 1901, produced the novelty topsy-turvy doll shown here. With this doll, children got two toys in one: with the swift turn of her skirts the toy transforms from a black, ragtime female dancer into a mohair teddy bear. The doll's face was first printed onto fabric and then pressed and stiffened into shape. The head is marked and dated July 9th, 1901. The teddy bear part of the toy is made of mohair and stuffed with excelsior. She has many typical features of other American bears from this period, including black shoe-button eyes and large ears set on either side of her head. These dolls are very rare today, and are popular among collectors because of their novelty design.

Height: 11in (28cm)
Approx value: $2,300

TEDDY DOLLS

Novelty bears with concealed doll faces were first made in 1906, to encourage little girls who usually played with dolls to play with bears. The example on the near left was made around 1910, and is very rare. The bear is fully jointed, is made of short mohair, and has shoe-button eyes. Although it was made in America by an unknown manufacturer, the celluloid doll's face was imported from Germany. The other example is a Billiken Doll, made by E.I. Horsman in 1908. The firm made a variety of novelty bears and dolls in the early 20th century, but they are best known for this doll. Their advertising describes it as "the merriest and jolliest of playthings." It came in many varieties and sizes, including a dressed example and a sister Billiken with a wig! The doll has a composition head and a mohair body.

Height: *left* 11in (28cm); *right* 11in (28cm)
Approx value: *left* $2,100; *right* $680

Teddy Doll, c.1906   Billiken Doll, 1908

LEFT Few of these stick bears survive in very good condition. This example is typical: he has only one remaining eye, which is made of metal. Other examples have black boot-button eyes.
Height: 10in (25.5cm)
Approx value: $125

MASS MARKET BEARS

After the First World War, a vast number of teddy bears were made by small toy manufacturers who have now faded into anonymity. These mass-produced bears do not share the high quality of the earlier bears made by such firms as Ideal, Hecla, and B.M.C. Because of their reduced features they have become known as stick bears. The heads tend to be unusually large for the size of the bear. Although made by a number of different firms, the bears share many characteristics, including short bristly mohair, small gathered ears, and a thick neck. Traditional and novelty examples were produced in many different sizes.

THE "ELECTRIC EYE" TEDDY BEAR

"Electric Eye" bears were produced by a number of American manufacturers at the beginning of the 20th century. However, the mechanisms quickly broke and few of the bears survive today. The American-Made Stuffed Toy Company of New York made their bears in three sizes—16 inches (40cm), 18 inches (45cm), and 22 inches (55cm)—and in a variety of colors. Other unidentified manufacturers also made the bears. A number of different methods were used to activate the lights in "Electric Eye" bears. On some examples, the flashlight bulbs in the eyes light up when a doorbell-like button concealed near the left ear is pressed—a stitched cross indicates the area to press! On others, the lights are worked by pressing an area in the bear's stomach. To replace the batteries the seam at the back of the bear has to be opened and then resewn—not the most practical of solutions! It is very rare for the lights on these bears to be working, and any examples that have eyes that still light up are particularly collectible.

LEFT AND RIGHT The patriotic "Electric Eye" bear on the right, made by The American-Made Stuffed Toy Company of New York around 1917, has red, white, and blue mohair. Like most "Electric Eye" bears, he has a stiff, unjointed neck and legs, but jointed arms. Other examples include the white bear, made around 1907, and the red bear, which was made a little later. Their mechanisms are all still working, which is rare.
Height: 22in (55cm) each
Approx value: $850 plus each

Knickerbocker

The Knickerbocker Toy Company was founded in Albany, New York, in 1869, to produce educational toys. The first teddy bears can be dated to around 1920, when Knickerbocker introduced permanent labels on their toys, but these bears are very rare today. The name "Knickerbocker" is taken from the nickname given to the Dutch settlers in New York who wore baggy knickerbocker trousers. From 1968 to 1977 the firm was licensed to produce Smokey the Bear for the American Forest Fire Prevention Campaign. They moved to new premises in Middlesex, New Jersey in the 1960s, and labels from after this time have the new address. The gift division of Knickerbocker, Applause, was sold in 1982 to Wallace Berrie (*see p.108*). Knickerbocker ceased business in the 1980s, when they were taken over by CBS Inc. Because the company continued to produce bears until the 1980s, and because their bears are well documented, they are easier to find than many other U.S. bears, and are popular with collectors worldwide. Identifying characteristics of Knickerbocker bears include separately sewn-in muzzles, a very wide head, and short snout, and paw pads made of velveteen. Some early bears have metal noses; others have conventional stitched ones. Bright gold, brown, and white mohair were the prevalent colors of the bears during the 1930s.

ABOVE Knickerbocker bears from the 1930s have characteristically narrow, thin, vertically stitched noses, and big cupped ears sewn across the seams of the face. Cinnamon or dark brown bears usually have contrasting light-colored paws. The pads on this example are felt, but many, especially later ones, are velvet. Muzzles are pointed, but not particularly long.
Height: 15in (38cm)
Approx value: $450

RIGHT The celluloid googly eyes of this 1930s bear are unusual for Knickerbocker. However, he has many other common Knickerbocker characteristics, including a small pointed muzzle and very large ears. The narrow, oval shaped nose with vertical stitching is typical of this period. The bear's growler inside his chest still in working order.
Height: 20in (51cm)
Approx value: $750

1930s vertically stitched nose, and very large ears set on the side of the head.

The alternative metal nose design featured on some 1930s Knickerbocker bears.

By the late 1930s bears had an inset muzzle made from a separate piece of material.

ABOVE Some 1930s Knickerbocker bears, such as the one shown here, have metal noses; others have metal eyes. The profile of this bear shows the typically flat body of pre-1935 designs. The pads are made of velveteen.
Height: 17$\frac{1}{2}$in (44.5cm)
Approx value: $450

BELOW This 1935 cinnamon bear is in pristine condition. His head is stuffed with wood wool to make it hard, and his body is stuffed with softer kapok.
Height: 20in (51cm)
Approx Value: $675

ABOVE A feature of later Knickerbocker bears is the inset muzzle of clipped mohair, introduced by the firm in the 1940s. This bear has a different type of nose stitching from that of many of the bears featured here, and is quite unusual because he has a felt tongue peeping from his mouth. Other bears from this period were made with felt noses. Unusually for Knickerbocker's darker bears, the pads are of a lighter color than the mohair. The muzzle is rounder than that of earlier bears.
Height: 21in (53.3cm)
Approx value: $900

ABOVE The wide head with large ears, inset clipped muzzle, velveteen pads, and high quality greenish-gold mohair are all typical characteristics of Knickerbocker bears from the 1950s. This bear has large amber glass eyes, and velvet pads in a contrasting dark color to the mohair. The flat body and head of Knickerbocker's earlier bears have now become much plumper (compare the profile of this bear with that of the 1930s example at the top of the page). Many American manufacturers started using less expensive synthetic materials in the 1950s. This bear is stuffed with polyfiber rather than excelsior.
Height: 17in (43.18cm)
Approx value: $450 plus

BELOW Dating from around 1937, this small Knickerbocker bear has a characteristic inset muzzle made from a separate piece of clipped mohair. He displays all the typical features of Knickerbocker bears from this time, including a wide, flat head, oval-shaped vertically stitched nose, amber and black glass eyes, narrow pointed muzzle, and very large ears set on the side of the head. He is in mint condition, and still has all his original felt pads. The Knickerbocker label stitched into his chest states that he was made in the United States and conforms to the country's sanitary laws.
Height: 14in (35cm)
Approx value: $350

ABOVE Knickerbocker introduced synthetic fabrics after the Second World War. This musical bear is made of white nylon plush and is stuffed with cotton. He is unjointed, but jointed bears were also made at this time.
Height: 14½in (37cm)
Approx value: $45

ABOVE By the 1960s some Knickerbocker bears were made in Korea—as stated on the label of this cotton plush example. His amber plastic safety eyes with lines radiating out from them are a typical feature of the later bears.
Height: 15in (38cm)
Approx value: $45

ABOVE Design changed little on Knickerbocker's modern bears. Apart from its long synthetic fur, this example from the 1970s is very similar to the bear on the left. Inset muzzles are now velveteen rather than mohair plush.
Height: 16in (40.6cm)
Approx value: $175

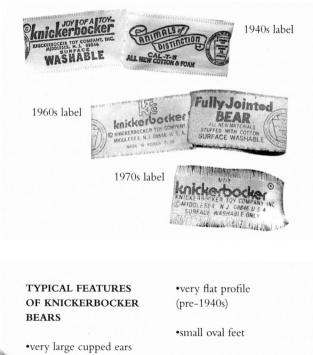

1940s label

1960s label

1970s label

TYPICAL FEATURES OF KNICKERBOCKER BEARS

•very large cupped ears

•clipped or shaved muzzle (late 1930s)

•very flat profile (pre-1940s)

•small oval feet

•no claw stitching

•vertically stitched nose

Gund

Gund Manufacturing Company was founded by Adolph Gund in 1898 in Connecticut, but moved to premises in New York City in the early 20th century. Initially a novelty and soft toy manufacturer, Gund began making teddy bears around 1906, although bears dating from before the 1930s are exceptionally rare. Adolph retired in 1925 and sold the business to Jacob Swedlin, who had started work in the factory as a janitor. Gund continued to expand its line of bears and novelties. In 1927 they developed their Jumping Animals under the trademark of Gee Line, and in 1948 they licensed and produced stuffed animals for Walt Disney, including Winnie the Pooh (*see p.149*). The factory moved to Brooklyn in 1950, and then to New Jersey in the 1970s. In 1979 they redesigned their stuffed bears and animals to attract adult collectors. They introduced their Bialosky bears in 1982. Gund's output is still flourishing, and like a number of manufacturers, some of their bears are now produced in the Far East.

RIGHT Teddigund was produced in the 1940s in different fabrics. This example is made from cotton plush and is fully jointed.
Height: 15$\frac{1}{2}$in (39.5cm)
Approx value: $100

ABOVE Cubbigund, an unjointed bear, made in rayon plush, or as seen here, cotton plush, was produced in the 1940s. This bear has a stitched nose, but some later ones had plastic molded muzzles. Like Teddigund, Cubbigund has movable googly eyes.
Height: 11$\frac{1}{2}$in
Approx value: $85

ABOVE Gund made several different pandas. This 1940s example is very similar in style to their teddy bears—made of cotton plush, unjointed, with very round ears, paws and feet, and the traditional googly eyes. Some later examples were made in synthetic fibers.
Height: 10in (25.5cm)
Approx value: $85

Applause Inc.

Applause produces a wide range of products, from stationery and ceramics to soft toys. They are known today for their high quality Avanti animals and Applause toys. Robert Raikes started to make artist bears with wooden character faces in the 1980s. The bears became very popular, and in 1985 Applause commissioned him to make bears exclusively for them. Raikes's bears before this time were made by his own hand and are particularly sought-after, but those first produced with Applause are also very collectible. The first series for Applause was made in a limited edition of 7,500 each, and sold out within three weeks!

LEFT Applause was a division of Knickerbocker Toys (*see pp. 104-6*) until 1982, when it was bought by Larry Ellis and Harris Toibb of Wallace Berrie & Company to form the Applause Division in 1984. They produced a range of animals, including this rather funny-looking monkey. Dating from 1981, his label is printed with "a division of Knicker-bocker." Made of synthetic plush, he is unjointed and has plastic eyes, and was clearly made for the mass market.
Height: 12in (30.5cm)
Approx value: $45

LEFT This "After Eight" bear was produced by Applause in 1986 after their merger with Wallace Berrie & Co. He is unjointed, made of mink plush, and has a leather nose.
Height: 17in (43cm)
Approx value: $35

RIGHT "Gracie" and "George" are typical of Robert Raikes's wooden-faced bears. They are both fully jointed and have artificial plush bodies and glass eyes. All these bears carry a Robert Raikes paper tag and have Raikes's name carved beneath one foot.
Height: 7in (18cm) each
Approx value: $100

RIGHT "Nicolette" is a special Christmas edition bear designed by Robert Raikes and produced in 1986 in a limited number of only 10,000. The face is typically hand carved, but the eyes are plastic rather than glass. She is fully jointed and made of acrylic plush.
Height: 15½in (39cm)
Approx value: $100

The North American Bear Co.

The North American Bear Company was founded in Chicago, Illinois, in 1978 by Barbara Isenberg. Among her very popular creations are Albert the Running Bear (the subject of a number of children's books she has written), the Very Important Bear Series, and the Vanderbear Family. The company not only produces unique and original bears, but also designs a complete range of high quality clothing and accessories for them to wear. They also make replicas of famous celebrity bears: in 1991 they produced a soft toy version of Aloysius for the television adaptation of the English writer Evelyn Waugh's novel, *Brideshead Revisited*.

FAR RIGHT The North American Bear Company's Very Important Bear Series was introduced in 1980. Each bear was based on a historical, literary, or celebrity figure, and their names are always a play on the word "bear." Four new designs are introduced each year, and are only available for a limited time, making them very collectible. LiBEARace seen here is a typical example, made of brightly-colored blue plush, and dressed in his glittering stage costume. **Height:** 20in (50cm) **Approx value:** $145 plus

LEFT When Albert the Running Bear was launched in 1978, he was a huge success. He came in various sizes and in different-colored outfits. Production was stopped in 1982, limiting the numbers and making Albert even more collectible. **Height:** 15in (38cm) **Approx value:** $65

LEFT The Vanderbear family is made up of many members, each with their own wardrobe of clothes designed by Odl and Katya Bauer. Muffy Vanderbear shown here is the baby of the family. She was introduced in 1984 and is still in production today. **Height:** 7in (17.5cm) **Approx value:** $35

RIGHT Humphrey BEARgart is another one of the North American Bear Company's Very Important Bear creations. Typically, he is dressed exactly in the character of the personality he represents. **Height:** 20in (50cm) **Approx value** $145 plus

Other Modern U.S. Makers

In the 1960s a number of American toy manufacturers started to have bears made in the Far East, where the cost of production was much lower. Sadly, this caused the fall of a number of old established firms such as Ideal and Knickerbocker, who were unable to compete with the new prices. Bears from the 1970s onwards tend to have been produced for the mass market. They are usually made of synthetic plush, although some limited editions are mohair. Probably most popular are those bears based on fictional or literary bears, or those made to commemorate a certain event. Retailers such as F.A.O. Schwarz often commission designs from the leading manufacturers worldwide, selling bears that capture the quality and character of vintage bears.

F. A. O. SCHWARZ

The F.A.O. Schwarz store in New York is one of the oldest and largest retailers of toys in the world. They opened their first outlet in 1862, and are now known worldwide for their beautifully decorated premises and high-quality toys. Many of the toys are commissioned from leading manufacturers, such as the German firm of Steiff, who produced The Golden Gate bear seen in the inset picture, developed to commemorate the opening of F.A.O. Schwarz's new store in San Francisco in 1989. Others include the American bear artist John Wright, who was granted exclusive rights from the Walt Disney Company to make Winnie the Pooh, Christopher Robin, and Piglet (*see pp. 148-9*). He produced a limited edition of 250 pieces for F.A.O. Schwarz in 1994, called Wintertime Pooh and Piglet, which are highly collectible.

RIGHT This huge bear, specially produced for F.A.O. Schwarz in 1993 is named "Truffles". This name was chosen because it was felt there could be no better thing to associate with a bear than the world's most popular chocolate confection. His synthetic fur is made to resemble old mohair.
Height: 29in (73.5cm)
Approx value: $150

RIGHT "Misha," an unjointed plush bear, was designed by the Russian artist Viktor Chizhikov for R. Dakin and Co., as the official mascot of the 1980 Olympic Games.
Height: 14in (35.5cm)
Approx value: $130

R. DAKIN AND COMPANY

R. Dakin and Company of California was founded by Richard Dakin in 1955 to import hand crafted items. They came upon soft toys by chance, when a number of them appeared as packing in a consignment of Japanese mechanical trains in 1957. Richard Dakin's son, Roger, who had just joined the firm, placed an order for them, and they were so successful that the firm began to design its own toys in the United States, known as Dream Pets. By the 1960s they had cut out their other lines completely to concentrate on their new product. The firm acquired a number of other toy manufacturers in the 1960s, and also began producing for Japan, Hong Kong, and Mexico. In 1989 they acquired the British-founded House of Nisbet. Among the firm's most popular lines are the American cartoon cat Garfield and his bear Pooky, the Pink Panther, and members of the Muppets.

Height: 15in (38cm)
Approx value: $30

Height: 8in (20cm)
Approx value: $30

THE COOPERATIVE FIRE PREVENTION'S SMOKEY BEAR

The Ideal Toy Company was the first manufacturer licensed to produce Smokey the Bear—the "spokesbear" for the Cooperative Forest Fire Prevention company—who made his first appearance on a poster drawn by Albert Astaehle in 1944. Since that time numerous highly collectible Smokey-related bears and toys have been made by companies that include R. Dakin and Co. and Knickerbocker. The example on the far left was produced by Dakin in 1970. He is made of hard plastic and has movable arms, but the firm also made plush versions. The bear's denim pants and plastic hat and shovel are all removable, and in some cases may now be missing. The plush bear on the near left was produced by Three Bears Inc. around 1985 and is typical of the plush Smokeys produced in the United States. He is unjointed and has an inset muzzle. His denim pants are sewn to his body. The first Ideal Smokeys had plastic faces, but later ones were plush.

AVALON INC.

Novelty bears with plastic molded faces are very popular in the United States. The example on the far left, made by Avalon Inc. of Pennsylvania in 1970, is known as the Thumb-Sucking Bear, for obvious reasons. His plastic thumb can be taken from his mouth whenever it gets sore! He is made of synthetic plush and filled with foam, and his features have been painted on his face. A cloth label sewn into his side identifies his manufacturer.

Height: 11in (28cm)
Approx value: $110

Height: 15in (38cm)
Approx value: $15

EDEN TOYS

Eden Toys produced bears from the 1970s onwards. They are frequently unjointed and have a soft filling. The brown and white bear shown here was made in around 1984 and is typical. This example can be identified by the tag sewn into his body. Eden Toys acquired the exclusive licensing and manufacturing rights to Paddington Bear in the United States in the 1980s.

Australian Bears

The mass production of Australian-made bears began in the early 1920s with the Melbourne (Victoria) firm, Joy Toys, and the Perth (West Australia) firm, Fideston Toys. Up until this time bears were imported into Australia from Britain.

These early Australian bears are of the highest quality, beautifully made of imported English mohair, and featuring exceptional glass eyes, and even at that early stage of production, uniquely Australian.

Between the 1920s and 1970s several firms were producing attractive bears for the home market. It is not known if any Australian-made bears were exported, but imported British bears were still sold in Australia. Firms making bears (and other toys) during this period include Barton Waugh, Berlex, Emil, Fideston, Jakas, Joy Toys, Lindee, and Verna. Import tariffs were lifted from imported toys in the late 1960s to early 1970s, and with the exception of Jakas, almost all Australian toy makers went out of business, as they could not compete with inexpensive Asian imports. Today, the teddy bear lover is well supplied again, with Australian-made artists' bears and the superbly crafted and uniquely designed teddies of a number of small new firms.

LEFT A 1930s Joy Toys bear playing on a swing with his friends.

RIGHT A rare Teddy-koala from around 1910. Originally he had a fur coat, but insect damage has resulted in a leather-look bear!

Joy Toys

Joy Toys started business in Melbourne, Victoria, in the early 1920s. This very energetic and imaginative firm made beautiful soft toys including dolls and bears. They made over 50,000 bears between the early 1920s and the 1960s, when Cyclops bought the company. The name Joy Toys is now owned by Toltoys, but was last used in 1976. Joy Toys made many styles of bears. Initially they were fully jointed, made from English mohair, filled with excelsior, and with their slim torsos and limbs, resembled German bears. By the 1930s the traditional Joy Toy bear "trademark" appeared, when the neck ceased to be jointed. It is not uncommon to find Joy Toy bears that have lost their original eyes, perhaps a fault in fixing the glass eyes in the factory. From the 1930s the bears resembled British ones, except for the stiff neck. Most had pointed upturned front paws. At this time they were filled with kapok. The nose stitching is very distinctive, with two longer outer stitches. Bears from the 1950s were filled with crumbed rubber and many weird and wonderful shapes have come about through the rubber perishing and falling to the bottom in a saggy lump. By the 1960s the quality of Joy Toys soft toys began to deteriorate, but earlier bears are highly sought after by collectors.

ABOVE This very early rare Joy Toys bear has a jointed neck and jointed limbs and is in good condition. The paw pads are twill cotton and he is excelsior-filled.
Height: 26in (66cm)
Approx value: $750

RIGHT Some Joy Toys bears produced before the Second World War had the long shaggy mohair of this 1930s gold example. His ears are set charcteristically wide apart and are quite far back on his head. He has the typical upturned nose stitches and pointed paws of Joy Toys bears from this period.
Height: 16in (40.6cm)
Approx value: $600

TYPICAL FEATURES
(1930s onwards)

•distinctive large nose with a long stitch running up at either end

•very short limbs and a large body

•unjointed neck

•pointed paws

•cotton twill pads

•mohair body

•short muzzle

The Joy Toys logo

A cardboard chest tag

1930s woven label

ABOVE This lovely 1940s Joy Toys bear has a stiff unjointed neck and typical nose stitching with longer outer ends, and pointed oil cloth paw pads. His glass eyes have been replaced. He is a rare cinnamon color and still has his label attached to his foot.
Height: 26in (66cm)
Approx value: $375

ABOVE This small cinnamon colored bear from the 1940s has lost his eyes, which is not unusual with Joy Toys bears. He is filled with kapok and his paw pads are made of rexine. Like many of the firm's bears, he still has his label on his foot.
Height: 11in (28cm)
Approx value: $225

ABOVE This 1940s bear started life with a long mohair coat with colored tips. His stiff neck, long outside nose stitches, and pointed paw pads are all typical characteristics of Australian bears. This little fellow has rexine paw pads and is stuffed with kapok.
Height: 16in (41cm)
Approx value: $300

ABOVE This beautiful 1950s bear has a stiff unjointed neck, long gold mohair, and excelsior and crumbed rubber stuffing, as well as the Joy Toys signature features: pointed paws and long outer stitches on the nose. He

still keeps smiling even though he has been in the washing machine and the dryer, and is in surprisingly good condition considering his treatment.
Height: 24in (61cm)
Approx value: $300

LEFT By the 1950s bears were filled with a mixture of rubber and kapok or rubber and excelsior. It is important to store these bears carefully, as otherwise the rubber perishes and the bear will collapse and look rather strange. Where the bears were left lying on their back, the rubber has set in a hard thick mass against the back of the fabric, giving the bears either no stuffing in the front or none in the back. The only course of action is to remove the perished rubber and restuff the bear. Luckily this one has managed to retain his original shape. Typically, he has an unjointed neck.
Height: 15in (38cm)
Approx value: $300

Other Australian Makers

Vintage Australian bears do not seem to have survived in any quantity, either in their native country, or outside. However, those that have are a highly prized addition to any collection of old teddy bears. While the bears being produced today in Australia come in many different shapes and sizes, the vintage Australian bear does have several uniquely Australian features. Happily, most old bears are labeled, making identification that much easier. In addition, most have characteristic upturned front paws, which almost come to a point in some cases. Unjointed necks are also a feature of many Australian bears (although very early examples were jointed). Another feature of early bears is the nose, which has a longer stitch on the outside, either going up, or going down—when it gives the bear a most serious expression!

LEFT AND RIGHT Lindee often used novelty designs—the 1930s bear on the left has a molded rubber nose. The bear on the right is almost identical but has a stitched nose. Because of their shape and the high quality of the mohair, early Lindee bears are often mistaken for English bears if the tags are missing.
Height: 20in (51cm) each
Approx value:
left $450; *right $600*

LINDEE
This most prolific soft toy making company was situated in a suburb of Sydney, N.S.W. from 1944 to 1976. The name was taken from the pet name used for Mr. and Mrs. Lindenberg by their staff. The firm produced beautiful dolls as well as soft toy animals of all sorts, including some on wheels. Lindee bears were made from English mohair, both fully jointed and unjointed, with lovely glass eyes, and brown vinyl paw pads. They were labeled with a printed cloth tag bearing a reclining fawn, and the words "Lindee Toys the Prestige Name in Soft Toys," sewn into the seam of the paw pad. Lindee bears have very large noses and mouths sewn in black. Some have exaggerated black claws. Lindee made bears until it went bankrupt in 1976, but those made after Mrs. Lindenberg sold the business in 1969 are of inferior quality.

LEFT This typical Fideston bear is made from tipped mohair and has leather paw pads. The head is typically large in proportion to the body. Excelsior-filled and fully jointed, these bears are very collectible. This beautiful example dates from the 1930s.
Height: 19in (46cm)
Approx value: $600

RIGHT These two very sweet Emil teddy bears date from the 1950s. Typically, they have a stiff neck, pointed vinyl paw pads, and noses with long outer stitches. Their bodies are mohair, and are stuffed with flock and excelsior.
Height: 14in (36cm) each
Approx value: $350 each

Height: 20in (51cm)
Approx value: $300

Height: 27in (69cm)
Approx value: $525

FIDESTON TOY CO.

The Fideston Toy Company was originally a Book and Music Depot, set up in Bunbury, Western Australia, by Richard and Louisa Fiddes. During the First World War, Mrs. Fiddes started to make soft toys as none were available in Australia. They became very popular, and in 1917 she fulfilled her first order, making her the earliest commercial teddy bear maker in Australia. In 1921 Fideston Toy Company was registered and a factory was established in a Perth suburb, mass-producing soft toys for stores in Australia. The business grew rapidly, employing 14 members of the family. By 1930 they were making a range of toys, but bears were most popular, with over 1,000 made a month. There were at least two designs, but only one is easy to identify, with a very broad head, large ears, and exaggerated cone-shaped muzzle. Until recently, Fideston bears were thought to be German due to their high quality.

EMIL PTY LTD.

Emil Pty Ltd. made bears and soft toys from the mid-1930s until the 1970s at various factories in and around Melbourne. The early Emil teddy of the 1930s and 1940s was made from imported mohair, with glass eyes, and either a jointed or stiff neck. The paw pads were oil cloth, the front paws are pointed, and the filling was a mixture of excelsior and kapok. The Emil nose is very distinctive, sewn in black thread, with two outside stitches that are longer than and go above the inner stitches. The bears are very handsome, with a broad head and wide-apart ears. By the 1960s, the quality of the mohair had deteriorated somewhat. All the bears now had a stiff neck; glass eyes were replaced by plastic and paw pads were white vinyl. However, the nose shape remained the same. Some Emil bears have black claws. The bears all had a satin label sewn into a back or side seam, printed with "Emil Toys Made in Australia" and a teddy sitting on the "E," but these are often frayed.

THE VERNA TOY COMPANY

The Verna Toy Company started business as dollmakers in 1941 in Victoria. They changed hands in 1948 and introduced teddy bears, to their wide range of dolls and toys. Bears before the 1960s were mohair plush and fully jointed, filled with excelsior, and traditional in shape. The most distinguishing characteristic is the blunt muzzle of the 1950s' bear shown on the far left here. Sometimes a felt nose was stuck onto the muzzle. From the 1960s foam rubber was used as the filling and bears had plastic safety eyes and vinyl pads.

BERLEX TOYS PTY LTD.

Berlex Toys was founded by Lex Bertrand in the early 1950s, making some of Australia's finest collectible old bears before going out of business in the 1970s in the face of competition from the Far East. Distinguishing characteristics of Berlex bears include the luxuriant mohair, big, well-shaped body and limbs, vinyl paw pads, and the triangular-stitched nose seen on the dressed lady on the left.

Japanese Bears

Vintage Japanese teddy bears are often made of poor-quality materials. Most early bears are made of short bristle mohair or blanket wool, rather than mohair plush. Many designs are similar to early American and French examples, with straight narrow bodies and limbs. They tend to be stuffed with excelsior. Feet are small and round and ears are made using the sliced-in method, by which the ear is pinched together and fitted into a hole in the head. Some bears are jointed, but again the joints tend to be of lower quality than Western examples, with cardboard discs often exposed on the outside of the limbs, and wire rather than metal used for jointing. Very few antique bears exist in Japan: not many were made, and most were destroyed during the Second World War. After the War, Japanese toy makers flourished as manufacturers of less expensive bears, exporting a wide variety of novelty bears to Europe and the United States. These are found in the greatest quantities today. From around 1950, the Japanese produced mechanical toys, including clockwork tin examples and traditional bears with mechanical devices. Teddy bears are becoming increasingly popular with the Japanese, and there are now stores, clubs, and museums devoted to them.

RIGHT This clown bear is typical of the novelty designs produced in Japan in the 1930s. Unfortunately he suffered a lot of damage: his short bristle body is now completely threadbare, and his cotton ruff is torn. He has only the remains of his mouth and nose and his felt paw pads are worn. However, his pink/green body and clown design still make him appealing. His construction is very basic, with the metal pins joining his arms and legs visible on the outside of the body. He has the characteristic sliced-in ears, gathered into a small hole in his head.
Height: 17in (43cm)
Approx value: $500

RIGHT Modern Japanese bears share many of the characteristics as earlier examples. These two small unjointed bears are made of synthetic fabric and are stuffed with foam. Their eyes are glass. They were made by the Japanese teddy bear artist Miuok Itu for a well-known Japanese teddy bear shop in Yokahama called Bruin's Bruin.
Height: 6in (15cm) each
Approx value: $30 each

ABOVE Certain characterisics suggest this early bear from the 1920s is Japanese even though he is not labeled. He is simply jointed with wires that go from the outside of the limbs all the way through the body; his ears have been attached using the sliced-in method; his body is made of short cotton plush, and he is stuffed with excelsior. An unusual addition are the red felt paw pads, but these may be replacements.
Height: 22in (56cm)
Approx value: $800

ABOVE In many ways this Yoski Pet is typcial of the inexpensive Japanese bears that were mass-produced after the Second World War. However, he is quite unusual because he has felt rather than glass or plastic eyes. Like a number of other bears produced in the 1940s and 1950s, he has a red felt tongue. His cotton clothes are sewn onto his body, and he has a embroidered label sewn into his arm.
Height: 10½in (27cm)
Approx value: $60

TYPICAL FEATURES OF JAPANESE BEARS

- mechanical or novelty design

- simple joints, often visible on the outside of the body

- unjointed (post-Second World War)

- short mohair or cotton plush (pre-Second World War)

- basic construction

- acrylic plush body (post-Second World War)

- inset muzzle of a different color from the rest of the body (post-Second World War)

- small sliced-in ears gathered into a groove in the head

MECHANICAL BEARS

Japanese toy makers produced many mechanical bears in the 1950s. Those shown here are typical examples. The bear on the near left has the name of the manufacturer—Alps—lithographed beneath his base. Battery-operated, the eyes light up as the bear pours himself a drink of milk. The other two bears pictured here are also battery operated. The one in the center of the group is doing her knitting; the one on the right is turning the pages of a book with his right hand. The mechanisms that work the bears are very basic: the reading bear has a magnet attached to his right hand which pulls up the pages and turns them over. Characteristic of Japanese mechanical bears, all these are unjointed and have metal bodies covered in nylon plush. The clothes of the reading bear are glued onto his body.

Height: 9½in (24cm)
Approx value: $195

Height: 6½in (16cm) each
Approx value: $150 each

Replica Bears

As old teddy bears become increasingly popular with collectors their price is rising. A number of manufacturers in the 1980s started producing replicas of their earlier bears that have all the nostalgic charm of the originals, but are far less expensive to buy. In many cases, the manufacturer has the original patterns to cut the new bears from, so many replicas are very faithful copies. Sometimes replicas are made of celebrity bears (Aloysius from the British series *Brideshead Revisited* is a typical example, reproduced by both The House of Nisbet in Britain (*see p. 15*) and The North American Bear Company in the United States), and these too are collectible. Replicas are often made in a limited edition, sometimes for a particular country or retailer. Such is their popularity today that some, particularly those made by Steiff, are themselves going for high prices. In general, however, replicas provide an opportunity for people with limited budgets to have in their possession a traditional-style bear made by a top manufacturer. Replicas are usually packaged in special boxes and are fully labeled, with a certificate giving details of the limited edition. If you take your bear out to display him, it is important to keep the box and the certificate in a safe place, because any collector's bear with its original packaging will command very high prices in the future.

LEFT In recent years Merrythought (*see pp. 68-71*) has produced a vast range of collector's bears, including limited editions, replicas and anniversary bears. They have also made modern versions of many of their traditional vintage bears, including the dressed Bingie line, Punkinhead, and the Cheeky bear. They have also produced a replica of Mr. Whoppit, the bear that accompanied world land and water speed record-holder Duncan Campbell on his dangerous journeys, surviving Campbell's last fatal attempt. Shown here on the left is a 1995 Cheeky replica. He is almost exactly the same as the 1960s version shown above—he has the same color golden mohair, glass eyes, felt paw pads, and an identical printed label on his foot.
Height: 14in (35.5cm)
Approx value: $60

LEFT Gebrüder Hermann produced this replica (*far left*) of their vintage 1930s teddy bear in 1994. Made in a limited edition of only 2,000, he has all the traditional qualities of the early bears, and Hermann has managed to capture all the original charm.
Height: 12in (30cm)
Approx value: $55

BELOW Teddy Clown was produced in 1986 in a limited edition of 10,000, as a replica of the original Teddy Clown Steiff introduced in 1925. Although his hat and ruff are virtually identical to the original (*inset*), the tipped mohair has been replaced by gold.
Height: 13in (33cm)
Approx value: $450

BELOW The original Alfonzo (*inset*) was an exceptionally rare red Steiff teddy bear given to Princess Xenia Georgievna in 1908 by her father, George Michailovich, the Grand Duke of Russia. The bear remained in the Princess's possession all her life, surviving the tribulations of her family, including the assassination of her father at the Peter and Paul Fortress in St. Petersburg in 1919. Princess Xenia died in 1965 and Alfonzo lived with her daughter until he was sold at Christie's in London to Ian Pout of Teddy Bears of Witney for a world record auction price. Steiff made a replica of Alfonzo especially for Ian's shop in 1990, in a limited edition of 5,000. These exact replicas have identical cossack outfits and have been traditionally hand-stuffed with wood wool. They are packed in a special presentation box and come with a full history of the original Alfonzo's troubled past.
Height: 13in (33cm)
Approx value: $400

Unidentified Bears

There are lots of wonderful vintage bears on the market whose makers are not known. It is usually possible to date the bears, and certain characteristics may point to a particular country of origin, but often the maker remains a mystery. Silver or china items may be stamped with a mark that is difficult to remove, but teddy bears often had paper tags that were taken off before they were given to children to play with. Similarly, the metal buttons used by Steiff and Bing were removed by parents for safety. Some collectors like to know who made their bear, and others insist there is a label or some form of identification before they buy a bear. But many collectors do not mind, they simply fall in love with a certain face and that's it. These lovely unidentified bears have a particular charm of their own and deserve a place in anyone's bear collection.

ABOVE The thick gold mohair coat and clear glass eyes of this bear suggest he was probably made in the 1930s. However, his country of origin is uncertain. He is still in excellent condition.
Height: 18in (46cm)
Approx value: $600–700

ABOVE These bears are probably English. The red boy dates from the First World War, and has replacement eyes. The short limbs and flat face of the girl suggest she is later.
Height: 14in (35.5) each
Approx value: *boy* $600–700; *girl* $75

ABOVE The fact that this bear is made of cotton plush suggests he was made after the Second World War. However, because a number of countries made this kind of bear, the place of origin is not certain.
Height: 12in (30.5)
Approx value: $550

ABOVE The vivid gold mohair of this bear was particularly popular in the 1920s and 1930s. His original felt paw pads have been replaced with cotton, but he is still in very good condition.
Height: 20in (51cm)
Approx value: $550–650

LEFT There are similarities between this black bear and those made by Steiff for the British market in 1912 (*see p.26*). However, Steiffs were copied by many makers and this bear's origins are unknown. His color is particularly desirable and will add to his value.
Height: 16in (41cm)
Approx value: $425

RIGHT Certain characteristics suggest that this bear was made in the United States in the 1930s. These include:
•distinctive nose stitching
•barrel-shaped body
•particularly bright mohair
•cotton paw pads
•short mohair
He has been dressed by his owner in modern clothing, possibly to protect him from further wear.
Height: 20in (51cm)
Approx value: $300–450

ABOVE The fact that the inside of these two bears' ears are of a different material from the rest of the body suggests the bears are French. Other French characteristics include the use of cotton and wool materials and the rather basic design.
Height: 15in (38cm)
Approx value: $150–250 for the two

Artist Bears

The first artist bears were created on America's West Coast in the 1970s, but artists from all over the world soon followed suit, and now many countries, including Germany, Holland, Britain, Japan, Australia, and France, all have famous bear artists. Bear artists design and make their own bears. They may employ outside workers, or family and friends may help, but the finishing touches will always be done by them. Successful artists must not only have good technical skills, to make the bear properly, but must also be very imaginative, to create a bear that is uniquely their own. Artist bears are usually produced in small limited editions, making them the collectibles of the future. Waiting lists are often long, and to overcome this problem, manufacturers such as Dean's in Britain have commissioned well-known artists to design bears exclusively for them, enabling them to be mass-produced. Artist bears can be bought at teddy bear stores, bear fairs around the world, or directly from the artist. Addresses of the artists featured in the following pages are listed in the Gazetteer at the back of the book.

LEFT A delightful collection of artist bears from all around the world.

RIGHT "Mademoiselle Fairy" by Japanese bear artist, Michi Takahashi.

Macbears, Melbourne, Australia

Rosalie Macleman was inspired to make bears when she was unable to find one she liked in Australia. She had a background in arts and crafts and found that making bears brought together all her interests and skills—designing, sewing, embroidery, leatherwork, woodwork, and a passion for the past. Rosalie was encouraged by friends and family to produce bears commercially, and so developed her Macbears. She showed them to the public at the Melbourne Doll show in Camberwell, Australia, and has won several awards. She uses only natural materials, usually camel hair and mohair—short pile fabrics that create defined lines. She makes all the props—clothing, satchels, boats, books—herself.

"A Bear and his Kite." Rosalie Macleman likes to combine all her skills in making her bears. This Macbear is dressed in his outdoor gear, including leather shoes and a duffle bag Rosalie made herself.

Nostalgia Bears, Melbourne, Australia

Deborah Sargentson started making bears only in 1993, after leaving her job as a Human Resource Manager. She was soon devoting most of her days and nights to producing bears and dressing them in old-fashioned clothing she made herself. She entered her first competition at the Malvern Teddy and Doll show, Australia, and won several awards. Several teddy bear shops wanted to stock her bears, and now the bears are finding homes throughout the world. In addition to standard editions, Deborah produces a limited number of private commissions each year, which can take over a hundred hours each to complete. Nostalgia Bears are known for their antique accessories—genuine gold spectacles, fob watches, and pipes.

Deborah Sargentson's Nostalgia Bears are based on traditional designs. This example, "Bear in a Garden," is wearing an antique smock and has a bow in her hair. Recently Deborah has added Grizzly bears and Pandas to her line.

House of Brook Bri, Adelaide, Australia

Briony Nottage's first bear was made of lambswool, but she went on to produce bears in a variety of other materials including sheepskin, mohair, and even sterling silver. But nothing prepared her for the difficulty she faced when making her first Barramundi fish skin bear! Briony was ecstatic when she came home to her family with what looked like a piece of old leather the cat had sharpened his claws on, but they were less enthusiastic. Not to be deterred, she couldn't wait to start designing a bear from this strange material. It was the biggest challenge she had ever faced! It took a whole day to pull through one leg after she had hand-sewn it, but it was worth it. Her weird bear soon gained a reputation and people came from all over Australia to look, smell, and touch it.

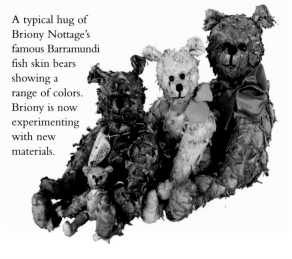

A typical hug of Briony Nottage's famous Barramundi fish skin bears showing a range of colors. Briony is now experimenting with new materials.

Heather Brooks' "Winston" closely resembles traditional-styled teddy bears. He is made of mohair and has glass eyes. Shown with him is "Pandy," a new addition to Heather's collection, also made of mohair.

Bearly Collectable, Mittagong, Australia

Heather Brooks creates her original artist bears under the name of Bearly Collectable. She started bear-making in 1986 and her bears are usually of a traditional design, with about half of them dressed in clothes she has made herself. Most of Heather's bears are one-of-a-kinds, or are made in limited editions of ten. Bearly Collectable bears have found homes in Germany, Britain, America, and Japan. Heather attends shows all around Australia and her bears have won many awards. Some of her favorite designs are baby and toddler groups and a panda she recently added to her collection. Heather enjoys meeting the people that collect artist bears, and she is delighted when her bears find a loving new home.

"Chadwick" is one of Lexie Haworth's special edition bears. Lexie uses traditional materials and finishes all her bears by hand. Like most of her bears, this example is undressed—she prefers to create the character through the facial expression.

The Bears of Haworth Cottage, Nowra, Australia

Lexie Haworth's interest in bears began in 1992, when at a local doll and bear show she discovered that a bear she had bought at a bric-a-brac auction was a 1905 Steiff. She went home and decided to make her own bears. She bought a commercial pattern, some acrylic fur and after hours of perseverance, her first bear was born. After a second attempt, she designed her own patterns, and hasn't looked back since. She now mostly uses mohair. The bears are machine-sewn, but they are all finished by hand. Most of her bears are undressed—she admits she isn't a terrific seamstress—and any that are dressed wear clothes made by colleagues. Lexie copies traditional styles, and tries to re-create the Steiff look.

"Jackie" is part of a group called "Camelot Remembered—A tribute to Jackie Kennedy," which included a pet dog and friend. She is wearing a 1960s blue coat and hat. On her lapel is a campaign button. A music box inside her body plays the tune *Camelot*.

New Mexico Paws, Baltimore

Susan Redstreake Geary has been making and designing her own teddy bears since around 1990. She started her business in New Mexico (hence the name), but has since relocated to Baltimore, Maryland. She had previously produced and designed original awardwinning art quilts for America's top quilt magazines. She specializes in character bears, and often equips them with props or pets. Although she produces over 250 bears a year, she manages to make them entirely by herself. Susan has been nominated for many prestigious teddy bear awards, including the Golden Teddy Award, and was a winner of the American National Teddy Roosevelt Bear Contest. In any spare time she has, Susan writes articles for a number of teddy bear publications.

Gloria Franks, West Virginia

Gloria Franks started making bears in the mid-1980s, after her husband had retired from the Navy and she had sold her travel agency business. Gloria used her previous experience of crafting cloth dolls to make and sell her own bears at local craft and trade shows. Her first designs were very traditional, based on antique bears she had come across at shows and auctions. Gradually her creations changed as her bears developed their own individual look. Many of her creations are large bears, which are easy to cuddle. Most of her bears are made of mohair, and many are dressed. They have been featured in a number of leading teddy bear magazines worldwide and have also been exhibited at several conventions.

"Young Bearon Franks" is one of Gloria's Teddy Toddlers, a series of child-size bears standing 30 inches (76cm) high and wearing toddlers' clothes and shoes. He is made of mohair and is fully jointed.

Stier Bears, Pennyslavania

Because Kathleen Wallace couldn't afford to buy the antique bears she loved so much, she decided to make her own. It took her a long time to produce a bear she liked, and she made several unsuccessful attempts. However, when she attended her first bear show in 1982 with her first 50 bears, they were so popular that they all sold out. Kathleen is a prolific seamstress, and has now made over 1,000 bears. She specializes in large bears, with the tallest so far standing at 45 inches (114cm). She produces limited editions of her bears for a number of stores, but makes one-of-a-kinds for her shows. She exhibits her bears not only in the United States, but also in Japan, Australia, and England.

"Bill" is fully jointed. He is made of honey-colored mohair and filled with pellets. He is fitted with a growler so that he can talk. Seated on his knee is "Webster," a butterscotch mohair bear.

Elaine Fujita-Gamble, Washington

Elaine Fujita-Gamble, a Washington State physical education teacher, began collecting bears in 1973 after she was given a bear as a gift by a friend. In 1979 she designed a pattern for some children she was teaching so they could make their own bears, and this sparked her bear-making career. Even though her first bear, based on an old German Hermann bear, was only 5 inches (12.7cm) tall, her bears have become progressively smaller, and are now usually around only 2 inches (5cm) tall. Because Elaine works full-time, she makes only small limited editions, and prefers to sell at shows. Her bears are renowned for their detail and fine workmanship and are in such high demand that they literally sell out within minutes of a show opening.

Tiny "Bedtime Ted" is only 1$\frac{1}{2}$ inches (6.35cm) tall. He was made especially for the 1994 Disneyworld convention in a limited edition of 25. He is wearing his bunny slippers and is carrying his blanket upstairs to bed.

Mary's passion for cats can be seen here. "Yvonne" is made of mohair, has glass eyes, and is fully jointed, with armature in her arms so she can hold her cat. "Treasure Kitty" is made of German synthetic fur and has a jointed head.

Mary Holdstad and Friends, Washington

Mary Holdstad has had an interest in handicrafts since her childhood, when as a young girl she would sit down with her older sister and draw paper dolls and sew clothes for her Barbie doll. After working in several different media, she bought a book on how to make teddy bears and has been hooked on her hobby ever since. Her passion for cats worked its way into her love for making bears, and in 1984 she launched her first cat-and-bear combination called "Katie's new Kitten," which earned her international acclaim. Since that time many of her bears have cat companions. The bears, which are made of high quality mohair, have won Mary many awards over the years.

"Tea Time Sweater Girl" is dressed in a very pretty outfit. Her sweater and shoes are hand-dyed, and her hat and purse are antiques. Made of mohair, she is fully jointed and has glass eyes. She has a typically sweet face.

Susan Horn Bears, Michigan

Susan Horn made her first bear in the early 1990s, and after several attempts she had enough bears to present at a show, where they were immediately successful. She now attends eight shows a year, and her popularity continues to grow as her bears display ever greater attention to detail. Susan uses vintage materials for her bears, or she ages new materials by dyeing them, to make them look and feel like old bears. In order to achieve a face that she was happy with Susan studied numerous photographs of vintage bears. The sweet face that she designed based on her research now complements all the bears she makes. She produces limited editions and one-of-a-kinds.

Apple of my Eye, New Hampshire

Frances Harper was already an accomplished seamstress when in 1990 she bought a *Vogue* pattern to make a teddy bear as a gift for a friend. The friend was so delighted with the bear that she urged Frances to make more of them. She has now made over 500 bears, and has left her 14-year career as a floral designer to devote herself full-time to bear-making. She researches antique teddy bears and bases her designs on these as closely as possible, using mohair for the body, and glass for the eyes. As with many other bear artists, Frances pays particular attention to the facial expression, and makes sure that none of her bears look too cute—she prefers them to be wistful or serious. She works on her bears for up to ten hours a day to keep up with the demand.

"Christopher" has a very serious expression. He is made of distressed mohair, is fully jointed, has wool felt pads, handblown glass eyes, and is stuffed with excelsior.

Hana Franklin, Toronto, Canada

It was not until Hana was thirty that she developed an interest in teddy bears. At the time, she had a career in banking and had started a gourmet cooking class in her spare time. A friend of hers, knowing about her passion for chocolate truffles, bought her a chocolate-brown bear named "Truffles" for her birthday, and from that time Hana fell in love with bears, collecting them on her various travels abroad. She soon started making her own. They are usually one-of-a-kinds, and she concentrates on giving them loving faces. They are made with imported mohair, which she often dyes for an antique effect. Many are dressed, either in clothes Hana has made herself, or in antique garments.

"Betty Buttons" is made of pink mohair

"Benjamin" has a wistful face

Fred Bears, Richmond Hill, Canada

Lesley Mallet inherited her sewing skills from her mother, a professional seamstress. She started making craft toys while awaiting the birth of her first child in 1978, donating the products to children, friends, and charities. This inspired her to collect bears, and at last count she had 320 in her house. She set up her business in 1992 and now makes around 100 bears a year, selling them at shows and stores in Canada, England, and the United States. She also runs workshops on how to make bears. Most of her bears have long legs and cuddly bodies. She makes every stage of the bear herself, from designing the pattern to brushing out the seams on the completed bear. She prefers simple accessories.

"Barnaby" is typical of Lesley's teddy bear designs, undressed and with few accessories. He has long limbs and his body is stuffed with pellets to give him a floppy appearance. He is made of German plush and has glass eyes.

Friendship Teddy Bear Factory, Markham, Canada

Cherie Friendship began making her bears in 1992 after she had given up her job as general manager of an electronics company. She ventured by chance upon a teddy bear store in Unionville and was persuaded by the zealous salesman there to purchase her first bear—for $300. Her husband was convinced that there was a market for teddy bears and she soon started making her own. The first was made from a commercial pattern, and as she admits herself looked more like a rat than a bear! She has now made over 200 bears, including some limited editions. She also sells packs for people to make bears themselves. Her bears are all fully jointed and made from mohair, which she distresses to create a vintage effect.

Very few of Cherie's bears are dressed. "Foster" is a new bear, but his distressed mohair makes him look like a vintage one. All Cherie's bears have a small Canadian flag pin in their ear and a label on the foot.

Joan's bears are always dressed and have accessories. "Maud" is made of old tan curly feather mohair, with leather pads, and black glass eyes. She is wearing a straw hat trimmed with brown velvet and flowers, a rayon fringed shawl, and a bead necklace.

Joan Rankin, Moose Jaw, Canada

Joan Rankin's interest in teddy bears was sparked by a visit to a local teddy bear store in 1987. She started collecting them with fervor, and was soon making them herself to raise money to buy more bears for herself. Following a visit to a teddy bear convention in Seattle, she started designing her own patterns, and replaced synthetic materials with real mohair. She has created several character bears, such as "Baxter Brown Bear," the subject of a number of stories she has written. She has also made a group of bears dressed as English ladies and gentlemen inspired by author Michele Clise's *Ophelia* books. Joan has written her own stories about them and built them their own "Bearington Manor."

"In the Fur" is one of a group of Nicola's bears which won the 1994 British Bear Artist Award for miniature bears. This is the mother bear, seen here in her fur coat. She is carrying a bag full of bears to a bear fair, and is accompanied by her child.

Tree Top Bears, Crewe, England

Nicola Perkins works part-time with children with special needs, but has been making bears in her spare time since 1992. Initially a hobby, it is now a full-time occupation. Nicola's love of dolls' houses and their miniature contents inspired her to make miniature bears. She specializes in producing small dressed bears, for which her mother designs and sews all the outfits and accessories, from teddy muffs and fur coats to tiny gollies and rabbits. She works in limited editions and one-of-a-kinds. The bears are made from upholstery fabric from the United States, and have Ultra suede pads. Eyes are onyx. The clothes are cotton, with silk, ribbon, lace, and fine cord accessories.

"Precious" is made of one-inch curly mohair. She has suedette pads which are lined so that the pellets can't be felt through the material. Like all of Frank's bears, "Precious" is not dressed—Frank prefers to create natural bears and does not like to hide their features.

Charnwood Bears, Loughborough, England

Frank Webster is one of the few male bear artists in the world. His first professional contact with teddy bears was as a repairer and restorer. After eleven years of looking after old bears Frank decided to start making his own, passing on the restoration part of his business to his wife, Sue, who writes about these bears for the British teddy bear magazine, *Teddy Bear Times*. In 1993, after Frank had been making bears for five years, he decided that because they had become so popular and were taking up so much of his time, he would devote himself to making them fulltime, which he has been doing ever since. Frank makes all of his bears himself, producing mainly limited editions, and apart from a very few, they are made of mohair.

Penny Chalmers, Surrey, England

Penny Chalmers began crafting bears when she came across a bear at a doll fair that she fell in love with but couldn't afford to buy. She already made dolls, and decided to try her hand at bears. She enjoys dressing her bears, especially in lace velvets and brocades, and antique fabrics. She tends to make her own clothes unless she sees an ideal outfit in an antiques store. Penny tends to produce one-of-a-kind bears, each with its own individual character, although she does make a number of limited editions. Penny's bears are made from American or German mohair and have boot-button eyes. Occasionally, she uses glass. Noses and claws are embroidered in cotton. All her bears are finished by hand.

Penny makes her bears in many sizes

Most of Penny's bears are dressed

Gregory Gyllenship, London, England

Gregory has collected soft toys for many years, but started buying teddy bears after he was given two for Christmas in 1988. He collected mainly new bears, but also a few vintage examples. Materials from these prompted him to start making his own bears. Such was his success that in 1993 he gave up his job in the city to concentrate on bears full-time. He works on his own, making about 20 bears a month. He rarely makes two the same at one time. His designs are largely based on wild bears, created in a traditional style, but with the addition of a tail. He uses German and English mohair plush. Eyes are glass, or when available, black boot-buttons. Stuffings range from wood wool to light and soft kapok.

Gregory uses long, shaggy mohair for his bears; these two are typical

Mister Bear, Leighton-on-Sea, England

Jennie Sharman-Cox's childhood love of old bears was reawakened after meeting the celebrated arctophile Peter Bull at his home on Paxos, Greece. Using her experience gained at art school and during her work for a large theatrical costume house, where she learned to pattern-cut, Jennie decided to embark on her bear-making career. In January 1990 she started her own company, Mister Bear, specializing in small, limited-edition traditional style bears, which are treasured by collectors from Japan and Europe to the United States. She draws on a range of colored mohairs for her bears, and whenever possible, uses old boot-buttons for the eyes. The bears vary in size, and most are made in limited editions or as one-of-a-kinds.

Jennie's bears are made from many different types of mohair

A war refugee with
her toy bear

The distinctive face
of Miss Marples

Jo Greeno, Guildford, England

Jo Greeno made her first bear in 1989, and since then has acquired a strong following among collectors worldwide. She has been presented with a number of prestigious awards and has made guest appearances at festivals in the United States and Japan. She specializes in one-of-a-kinds with cartoon-like faces, large close-set eyes, and smiling mouths. She dresses her bears carefully, and gives them accessories to create the distinctive characters that have become her trademark. One of her famous bears is "Miss Marples," one of a pair of bears made under the title "Murder at the Vicarage," based on characters in the novels of the English crime writer Agatha Christie.

"Winterburn" is a
rich deep color

"Shortcake," an
ivory mohair bear

Bo Bears, Buckingham, England

Stacey Lee Terry established her bear-making company in 1988, and since that time has designed every bear herself, taking her inspiration from wild bears. She has produced a number of one-of-a-kinds and limited editions, and has supplied several celebrities with bears, including racing driver Nigel Mansell, dress designer Laura Ashley, and H.R.H. Prince Charles. These are all inspired by the very high demand for bears dressed as a member of a particular profession, such as a policeman or nurse. Stacey uses an industrial machine to construct the body of the bear, but the rest is finished by hand. Her bears are mainly mohair with glass eyes, and hand-embroidered noses.

Joan's "Grandad Grey" is seen here sitting in his favorite chair. His legs and arms have a distinctive bend in them so he can sit down. Made of gray mohair, he has black glass eyes, and his body is filled with pellets. His paw pads are made of leather.

Craft T Bears, Innishannon, Ireland

Joan Hanna has always liked soft toys, and as a child was encouraged by her parents to make them for charities and as presents. After doing some research into the possibility of a market for collectors' bears in Ireland, Joan decided to make her bears professionally. She sells them in stores in Ireland, where they are mainly bought by visitors to the country. She also sells by mail order, and since 1993 has started attending bear fairs in England. She began by using commercial patterns but soon created her own designs. She makes them all herself, with her family occasionally cutting out the patterns and making accessories. She tries to use traditional Irish fabrics wherever possible and has made several limited edition Irish theme bears.

Marcelle Goffin, Rouen, France

Marcelle Goffin began making old fashioned bears as a hobby in 1989, and her interest today is still for pleasure rather than business. Her first bear was cut from an old British Hugglets pattern. However, as her love for French bears deepened, she decided to base her own bears on those she particularly loved and so created her own designs. At one time she even produced replicas of famous French bears. Marcelle never uses the same pattern twice—each bear is created on the spot, and she adapts the design according to the materials she is using at the time. She particularly likes working with mohair, with glass for eyes. Most of her bears are undressed, because she does not want to hide their character.

Pictured here are two of Marcelle Goffin's 1995 bears. "Oskar," on the left of the picture, is a chocolate-brown mohair bear. His small companion on the right, "Plume," is made of distressed English beige mohair. Both have glass eyes.

Aline Cousin, Noisy le Grand, France

Aline Cousin began making bears in 1991. Finishing her first bear "Théodore" was a long process, since she had no experience—she worked on him for two months! To find out how make him she bought herself an old threadbare bear with its cardboard joints showing through to examine. She also studied photographs, to see what style of bear she wanted to create. Her first attempt was not a great success—the arms and body were too long and thin and she hadn't incorporated in the back the essential hump that she so much liked. However, she didn't give in, and finally produced "Théodore," whom she wouldn't let out of her sight! Since then Aline has made many successful bears.

"Berlington" was made in a limited edition of 25 in January, 1995. The first of the edition was made for the Louvre, Paris, and is housed in the Musée des Arts Decoratives. He is made from distressed cinnamon mohair and has wooden joints.

Marylou Jouet, Rennes, France

Marylou Jouet was already a fine patchworker when in 1989 she decided to make her first bear, a "*Patchours Spécial Noël*," from American cloth samples. Marylou's *Patchours* (Patchwork bears) have now become her specialty. Each one can incorporate between 150 and 260 different cloth samples. Since 1991 Marylou has also been producing a line of miniatures, and she also makes a number of mohair bears. Many of them have detailed handmade accesories, including silk ties and lace collars. The bears are stuffed with wood wool and are fully jointed. She uses only glass for the eyes, or in the case of her patchwork examples, antique boot-buttons. Each bear has a label that serves as his "adoption certificate", giving details of the edition of the bear and when it was made.

"*Patchours Multicolour*" is made of over 250 pieces of material. He was produced after the success of her Christmas bear, who had only 150 pieces of cloth.

"Roderick"

Award-
winning
"Fawzy"

"Lars", "Lotjr," and "Mitch"

"Bettina"

"Bachelor"

Just For You, Keerbergen, Belgium

Jean Van Meeuwe Slater started collecting antique dolls in the 1970s, and recently began collecting teddy bears. She made her first bear from a store-bought pattern, but disliked its flat inexpressive character so much that she decided to design her own. After many experiments she finally came up with a design she was happy with. She pays particular attention to the bear's face, and it can take her up to two hours to fashion the nose on a large bear! She makes only one bear at a time, averaging one to two a day. She rarely dresses them, although some wear antique lace collars. She uses mohair for the bodies and Ultrasuede for paws and pads. Noses are stitched and the eyes are glass.

Jane Humme, Bodegraven, The Netherlands

Jane Humme began making bears in 1986, although she had been producing all sorts of crafts from the age of six. Her interest in bears started when she was collecting antique dolls, and the fairs she attended also sold antique teddies. She decided it would be interesting to try to reproduce the features of these old bears in modern examples. At first she made the bears just for herself and her friends, but soon interest was so great that she began selling them. Jane makes all her bears on her own, and only produces small limited editions or one-of-a-kinds. Her favorite designs are those based on the classic traditional-style bears, with a long snout, a humped back, long arms, and large feet.

Boefje Bears, Haarlem, The Netherlands

Annemieke Koetse received her first bear for Christmas in 1949, when she was a baby. This toy soon became her friend, and by the age of four she had already knitted its first pair of trousers. She then made her bear some clothes out of material and from this developed her interest in dressmaking. As a young girl she designed and made her own clothes, and when she left school she chose fashion as her career. The memory of her early bear always haunted her, and in 1987 she made her first bear. By the fourth, bear-making had become her passion. Annemieke often uses unconventional methods, including boiling the bear or drying the fur at a very high heat. Most of her bears are mohair. They are all fully jointed, sometimes even in the wrists and ankles.

Pink Dino Bears, Konolfingen, Switzerland

Karin Koller started collecting bears in 1991, after falling in love with a Nisbet teddy bear she saw at a toy fair in Switzerland. When she visited England with her husband René in 1993 they went to a bear museum and were overwhelmed by the range. The couple particularly liked artist bears, which were not widely available in their country, so Karin decided to make her own. Her first bear was in pink plush, because mohair was difficult to find in Switzerland. But Karin and René soon began to experiment. People saw their bears and fell in love with them, and the couple now sells their creations regularly at a craft market stall as well as through other outlets in Europe.

"Ueli" was made by René
and wears clothes by Karin

Karin Kronsteiner's Künstlerbären, Graz, Austria

Karin started collecting bears in 1990, and produced her first bear—Petzi—in 1992. Only five months later she had her own bear show in her hometown of Graz, Austria, which brought her a great deal of publicity. She has now designed 45 different bears. She has just had her third show, and her bears have been featured on television and in the newspapers. Each bear is individually made by Karin herself. She designs all the patterns, buys all the materials, hand-sews each bear, and knits the clothes. Each bear takes between 30 and 50 hours to make, with the larger ones taking around 100 hours. They are all made from mohair, are jointed, have glass eyes, and are filled with synthetic materials and pellets.

"Dennis" was made in a
limited edition of only 10

Drüne Baren, Schwalbach, Germany

Heidrun Winkler has collected bears since childhood, and when her mother-in-law started making bears she soon wanted to as well. She designed her first pattern in 1992, and since then has created many shapes: short and long noses, small or big feet, bent or straight legs, but always with happy faces. She uses English mohair, alpaca, German cotton plush, and very occasionally, synthetic materials. Paws are made of felt, Ultrasuede, or leather, and eyes are glass. She is now experimenting with growlers, musical boxes, and movements. The bears are made in limited editions of between five and 20, and such is the demand that she works on them full-time, fashioning everything herself. She supplies to stores in Germany, as well as Europe, Australia, and the United States.

"Sunny,"
Heidrun's first bear

"Kasmir" has a distinctive shaved muzzle

Ineke decided to make this bear a boy. "Sir Frederick" is made of a very soft cream merino-wave distressed mohair, and is wearing one of Ineke's favorite scarves! His paws are made of matching goatskin. He is one of a limited edition of three brothers.

"Polli" is a unique bear

Both of these bears are made of short pile cotton velours and dressed in some of Mary's typical types of outfits. Sailor suits are also popular costumes. The small, sitting bear shown here is called a button bear because he has leather button joints.

Ineke's Teddybären, Munich, Germany

Ineke started collecting bears in 1990 and, so that she could repair them, enrolled in a bear-making course. This fired a passion in her, and she has been making bears ever since. She was soon creating her own designs, and in the case of her dressed bears, designing their clothes too. Each bear is hand-sewn and made from the best quality mohair or plush. They usually have black hand-blown eyes and black embroidered noses. The character of each bear is determined after it has been made; it is only then that Ineke decides whether it is male or female, and what clothes it should wear. Each bear is a limited edition, and even though no more than five of one design are ever made, no two are exactly the same.

Teddys by Vera and Verena, Neunkirchen, Germany

Vera and her daughter Verena have always enjoyed making handicrafts. Vera attended a bear-making course in Germany, and started to make bears to sell at small doll fairs. When Verena was badly injured in an accident she decided to make teddy bears for a living, and since that time the mother and daughter team has made hundreds of bears, selling them at markets and fairs, and attending competitions. Vera and Verena now have a mail order business. They produce one-of-a-kinds, preferring to sell them exclusively to one customer or store. They use very high quality materials and dress the bears in lavish costumes, and often make them their own little toys to play with.

Bear Basic, Cape Town, South Africa

Mary Kelly began making bears as gifts for friends, but she was soon running a business from home. She opened her very successful Bear Basic shop in Simons Town in 1990, which she now runs with her daughter and a close friend. They specialize in making old-fashioned teddy bears based on traditional designs, and also run a bear hospital. Mary and her daughter design all their own patterns. They make their bears from a velour cotton upholstery fabric and an imported acrylic golden fur pile. They also occasionally use mohair, but this is difficult to obtain in South Africa. The bears come in a variety of different sizes and have movable joints, sewn-through glass eyes, hand-embroidered mouths and claws, and felt paw pads and noses.

Miyuki Bears, Ashiya-City, Japan

Miyuki Wada was inspired to make bears in 1983, when her husband returned from the United States with a bear for her. Her first bear, made for her baby, had a body of yellow toweling and wooden buttons for its joints, and a small music box in its tummy, which her baby loved. She has now created over 400 different designs, working on them late at night when her children are asleep. When a bear is completed, it is allowed to spend the first night with her children in their beds. Miyuki's bears are all made from high-quality materials, including cotton plush and European mohair, which makes them particularly collectible. Many, like those shown here, have clothes and accessories.

"Popo"   "Percy"

Mammie Bears, Tokyo, Japan

Mayumi Watanabe began making her bears in 1990 when she was only 17 and still at high school. She bases her designs on vintage bears but then adds her own personal touches, spending a particularly long time on the faces. She has won many prizes both in Japan and the United States. Mammie Bears have traditionally long limbs, and, wherever possible, are made with antique mohair fur, ribbon, and eyes. They are stuffed with wood-wool (excelsior). Mayumi believes her bears look their best if they are left undressed, and few have accessories. Beacause Mayumi is still a student, she can make her bears only during her vacations. Consequently, numbers are limited, and each bear is especially precious to her.

"Gloria"   "Miriam"

Fairy Chuckle, Kanagawa, Japan

Michi Takahashi and her husband Hiro fell in love with a beautiful teddy bear they saw in a store window while on honeymoon in Vienna in 1988. The bear inspired Michi to try and produce her own bears from mohair, which she imported from the United Kingdom and the United States. She designs all her own patterns and sews all her bears by hand. Each takes around three days to make, but some special designs can take up to a month. All her bears are made in limited editions, and sometimes as one-of-a-kinds. Hiro produced his first bear on the couple's third wedding anniversary. He uses the same methods as his wife, but unlike Michi's bears, his bears are not dressed. Instead, Hiro concentrates on varying details, such as embroidery on the nose.

Hiro made these lovely bears in a limited edition of only five

"Lady Fairy" is one of Michi's award-winners

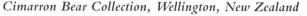

Here Cimarron's award-winning bear, "Captain Cook," can be seen charting the islands of New Zealand. He is fully dressed in period costume, and is shown holding a map standing in front of the country's national flag.

Cimarron Bear Collection, Wellington, New Zealand

Wanting a change from her career in Hotel Management, Cimarron Lang decided to sell dressed bears. She couldn't find any undressed bears she liked, so she made her own. All her bears are her original designs and are handmade. They range in size from 6 inches (15cm) to 35 inches (90cm), but the most common size is 16 inches (40cm). Her bears have mohair fabric, traditional glass eyes, wooden joints, felt pads, embroidered noses, and a distinctive hump. Most are filled with wool flock or pellets, and dressed in historical costumes, which Cimarron researches herself. She has created a number of character bears, and has also produced a number of teddy bears scenes, including "The Painters and Decorators."

Janis Harris's "Sir Ed Ted" is wearing a label which has been personally signed by Sir Edmund Hillary. His hat is a replica of what has become Hillary's lasting trademark. He is made of distressed mohair and has cotton clothes, and leather boots.

Almost South Pole, Auckland, New Zealand

Janis Harris originally made dolls, but has been making bears since the 1980s, and is now one of the longest-standing bear artists in New Zealand. She particularly likes making one-of-a-kinds and limited editions. Her bears are modeled on traditional designs. Most are made from mohair, but she also uses other vintage fabrics such as alpaca, wool, and antique rugs. In order to create an aged look, she also uses distressed mohair, which she hand-dyes to the color she wants. One of Janis's particular favorites is Sir Ed Ted (*see left*), which she designed in honor of New Zealand's famous explorer Sir Edmund Hillary, the first man to climb Mount Everest. Janis produced the bear in a limited edition of 26.

Frances's delightful twin bears

Braidwood Bears, Frankton, New Zealand

Frances McCleary began making teddy bears in 1990, initially using a pattern book, but then creating her own individual designs. She produces mainly one-of-a-kinds or small limited editions, concentrating on only one bear at a time to achieve greater individuality. Sometimes the bears wear only a bow, but at other times they are elaborately dressed in clothing hand-made by Frances. Her husband makes accessories for the bears, such as wooden rakes or sail boats. The bears vary in size from 8 inches (20cm) to 24 inches (60cm). They are all fully jointed with wooden joints, and have suede paw pads. Frances uses a variety of different fabrics to achieve certain effects, and particularly likes luxury mohair. All her mohair bears have glass eyes.

Bear Tales

Finding a bear with a record of its complete family history is not only very exciting, but also provides the purchaser with proof of its provenance. Knowing who owned a bear, where the bear has traveled, and the adventures it has had adds considerable charm. Often the vendor can provide the purchaser with information on the bear's family, and if you are very lucky there may be photographs of the bear with its owner. Many bears have become famous because of who owned them or because of something they have been involved in—the bear that survived the sinking of the Titanic is one we will probably all remember. A particularly well-documented or famous bear will solicit a great deal of interest and may as a result become extremely collectible. A perfect example of this is Colonel Henderson's cinnamon Steiff, Teddy Girl, which recently sold at a London auction house for a world-record price. Bears produced to represent a charity are also collectible.

Bill the educated bear

Bill is not only an extremely educated bear, he is also a very rare Steiff. He stands at 20 inches (51cm) high and has a long curly mohair coat. He was owned by an English family and given to the oldest child, Reginald by his grandparents in 1907 for his

first birthday. Reginald's brother, Esmond was born in 1908, and their sister, Althea in 1917. Reggie and Esmond took the much-cherished bear everywhere with them, including to Harrow School in 1919 and to Eton in 1922. The bear furthered his education at Oxford and Cambridge Universities before being passed reluctantly to Althea, who dressed him in fancy clothes and took him riding in a baby buggy. He was put into retirement between 1925 and 1955 and was then passed on to Esmond's grandchildren in 1957, traveling everywhere with them until it was decided in 1972 that the treasured bear should be passed on to a collector to take his proper place in rare bear history.

Tarquin the RAF mascot

When this bear was bought at an auction house in Lincolnshire, England, all that was known of him was that he had been the mascot of an R.A.F. squadron. During the Second World War there were many airfields in England but although a photograph of the bear appeared in the local paper, no one came forward with any information. Tarquin has great character and someone has made him a flying suit, adorned with various R.A.F. badges. Completing the outfit are a pair of over-large Wellington boots, and his original Second World War radio earphones and leather flying helmet. The silk cravat lends a rakish finish to the outfit. Tarquin was bought as a present for the British novelist Jack Higgins, who has a large collection of Second World War memorabilia. He discovered that the bear had come from Douglas Bader's Squadron, stationed at Lincolnshire during the war, but how he came to auction will probably always be a mystery.

Lt Col. Bob Henderson and his bears

Colonel Henderson's passion for bears began as a small child when he was given his brother's center-seam Steiff, Teddy Boy (*below left*). His interest continued throughout his childhood, and even when he served in the Royal Scots Regiment he carried a small bear in his tunic pocket. Retirement from the army allowed him time to become a true arctophile, and over the years his collection grew to include 500 bears that gradually took over his Edinburgh home. Teddy Boy was given a dress when presented to Colonel Henderson's daughter, and as Teddy Girl she accompanied the Colonel on his trips around the world. Upon the Colonel's death his bears were shipped over to Australia to be with his grandson, and in 1994 they were sold at auction in London. The fame of the Colonel's massive collection led to Teddy Girl selling for a record price of £110,000 ($165,000). The Colonel's lifelong companion, she was not only the inspiration for his bear collecting but also for that of many other devoted bear-lovers worldwide. Another of his favorite bears was Boots, named after his heavy boots, shown (*below right*) posing with the Colonel himself.

Libearty bear

Paul Fagan of Colour Box Miniatures was commissioned by the World Society for the Protection of Animals to produce this special bear for Libearty, the World campaign for bears. It is one of a number of tiny bears made by Fagan, many based on real teddies Paul has bought at auction over the years. Each bear is modeled by Fagan in Plasticine and then cast in resin, hand-painted and packed into a box with its own story. Libearty bear carries the story of the campaign and was made to raise public awareness about real bear species endangered by extinction.

A war-time bear

In 1932 a little boy who lived in Paris was given a beautiful teddy bear for his birthday. He called him Rosemousse after a popular waltz. The two were inseparable, growing up and sharing adventures together. During the Second World War, the boy's family fled from Paris on a cart packed with their possessions. To the boy's puzzlement his bear was lavished with love and attention by his parents on the journey, and it was only later that he discovered why: his bear had been carrying the family's fortune in his tummy.

Tubby bear

Tubby bear, a beautiful 28-inch (71cm) blond Steiff, was given to a little girl named Diana Bellenden Clark in 1912 by her father, a well-known actor of the day. Tubby was her constant companion, playing in the garden in Hayling Island and accompanying her everywhere—even sharing donkey rides when she went on vacation. When Diana became a nurse in a London hospital, Tubby was there, and when she was old and in poor health, he could still be seen sitting by her side in the nursing home where she was staying. Tied around his neck was a large label on which Diana had written that if anything should happen to her, Tubby was to go to her stepson, and the words, "We have been together since she was four." When Diana died, Tubby lived with the stepson for a while, and is now living happily in Sue Pearson's house.

Little bear

Little Bear is a lovely apricot blank-button Steiff (see right). He was a gift of a Colonel of the Manchester Regiment to his wife in 1910 before he was posted to South Africa, to remind her of her "Big Bear" (the Colonel was six foot four inches/1.9m tall). His wife took her Little Bear everywhere with her. He was with her during the births of her five children and comforted her after the death of two of her sons in the Second World War and the death of "Big Bear" himself. Not surprisingly, Little Bear was also with her when she died, aged 92. However, Little Bear is not lonely as he now lives in a new home and is ready to follow the lives and loves of a new family.

Portrait bear

It is rare to find paintings with teddy bears in them, especially appealing bears that are accompanied by an attractive portrait of their owner, and it is even more unusual if the owner is of interest because he or she is famous or particularly well-drawn. As a result, any painting that features an

attractive portrait and an endearing bear will always be greatly sought-after and command a premium when offered for sale. When the painting shown here appeared at auction recently, it generated much excitement, more so when it was realized that the very next lot was the bear itself! The auctioneers were persuaded to sell the lots together and they remain so to this day. The bear is probably German and from not earlier than 1910, the date of the painting. He was in a rather sorry state when he was bought, with moth-eaten pads and no eyes, but after a little care he soon looked like his old self.

The Three Musketeers

Ted, the large Steiff at the back of this group, came to England in 1907, and during the First World War spent his time in Liverpool with his owner and her sister Esme, comforting them as they shuddered in fear in the air raid shelters. The little girl (in the photograph below) died of cancer when only very young, but the bear stayed with her sister Esme all her life. He spent a lot of time in a canteen she ran for servicemen from all over the world, and was a great favorite with the Americans, often making up the numbers when the unlucky number of 13 sat down to tea. Unfortunately he was over-zealously washed and when he was bought by his present owner he had a thick stain from soap across his eyes and nose, the top of his head was completely bald where his hair has been scrubbed away and his stuffing had congealed into a solid lump. His two friends have been with him for over 60 years. The Alpha Farnell bear was Esme's neighbor's little boy's bear. When he went to join the RAF during the Second World War he left the bear in Esme's capable hands, but sadly he was never to return. The dog is an overnight bag named Wowie. Esme always kept a packet of chocolate Smarties inside him for visiting children. Having been through so much together, Ted, Alpha, and Wowie have become as inseparable as the Three Musketeers themselves.

Blinky Bill

In Australia the koala bear probably takes the place of the teddy bear in the hearts of many. The first Australian literary bear was Billy Bluegum, a koala bear created by Norman Lindsay, one of Australia's most famous writers and illustrators, that was featured in the Australian magazine, *Bulletin*, in 1904. He was rechristened Bunyip Bluegum for Norman Lindsay's children's book, *The Magic Pudding*, published in 1918. By the 1940s another literary koala bear, Blinky Bill, had overtaken him in popularity. Blinky Bill was a cheeky koala created by Dorothy Wall. Soft toy versions of him were produced, including the example on the right, made under copyright to Angus and Robertson in the 1970s.

Paddington Bear

Michael Bond wrote his first Paddington story about the bear he had bought his wife for Christmas. The couple had named him Paddington because they lived near the Paddington train station in London at the time (a 45-inch/114cm tall bear has honored the site since 1978). The tale was not initially conceived as a children's story—Bond was simply writing for his own pleasure. However, after ten days he discovered he had written a book. *A Bear Called Paddington* was published in Britain in 1958, and within a few years the adventures of Paddington were being read in England, the United States, and throughout the world. Bond produced a book a year until 1981. He also wrote television and film scripts for his bear, and regular five-minute episodes of *Paddington* were shown on British television, just before the early evening news. An animated cartoon series was recently created by America's Hanna Barbera, and Bond is still being approached by people who want to commit his bear to film. So keen was the demand for Paddington related products that Bond set up his own company to merchandise the bear, producing hundreds of related items. Merchandising is now being controlled by someone else, but output is still high. British designer, Gabrielle Clarkson, created the first soft toy version of Paddington in 1972, and has since produced Paddington's relative, Aunt Lucy. She held world exclusive rights to the Paddington Bear until 1976, but now supplies solely to Britain. In the U.S. Paddington has been produced by Eden Toys since 1975.

LEFT This Blinky Bill book is a pop-up version—when the pages are opened Blinky pops out of the book. It was published by the Whitman Publishing Company in 1935.

ABOVE This rare jointed koala was advertised as Blinky Bill when it was made by Morella Fur Toys. Made from kangaroo hide he is filled with sawdust. He has a large rubber nose and claws and beautiful glass eyes. Toy koalas were not labeled. It is rare to find early toys made from kangaroo skins as they do not stand the test of time unless stored well.

LEFT This large Paddington was made in England, by Gabrielle Designs. The U.S. version is much softer, and does not wear Wellington Boots. In 1982 Eden Toys' license was extended to the rest of the world, excluding Britain.

Rupert Bear

The Rupert Bear comic strip character made his first appearance in the British newspaper, the *Daily Express*, in 1920. He was created (as a rival to the *Daily Mail*'s cartoon character, Teddy Tail) by Mary Tourtel, a children's book illustrator and the wife of an editor on the newspaper. Rupert was an immediate success, and by 1932 there was even a Rupert League devoted to the bear. After ten years Tourtel was suceeded as illustrator by Alfred Bestall, who continued to work on the comic strip until the 1980s, when he was in his nineties. Books and annuals followed and the comic tales were translated into many languages, and soon this lovable British bear found a place

ABOVE British manufacturer Merrythought produced this version of Rupert Bear and his friend Bill Badger in the 1990s in a limited edition of 10,000 each.

RIGHT The Northampton-based firm of Burbank Toys produced a number of Rupert Bears in the 1960s, including this version with black and brown eyes and cotton waste (sub) stuffing.

FAR RIGHT Pictured here is a selection of Rupert bears, including, in the center, a musical roly poly bear, and, on the right, a glove puppet. The seated bear in front of the puppet has a synthetic body, and plastic hands and head. The standing bear is rubber. All are sporting Rupert scarves and checked pants.

in the homes of thousands, not only in Britain, but as far away as Japan, Australia, and New Zealand. The design of Rupert—an almost human-like bear with checked trousers and scarf and a woolly jumper— has altered very little over the years. He has been reproduced in many forms—there are soft toys, wooden puppets, books, plates, tins, postcards, and even Rupert Bear slippers. However, soft toy versions of Rupert were not made until the 1960s. Among those manufacturers producing Rupert Bear are Merrythought and Pedigree Toys in Britain, and Real Soft Toys in the United States. A cartoon series appeared on British television in the 1970s, and a video was released in 1984. There is also a collector's club, established in 1985, which has over 600 members worldwide and a quarterly publication, the *Nutwood Newsletter*.

Winnie the Pooh

"Christopher Robin gave a deep sigh,
picked his Bear up by the leg,
and walked off to the door,
trailing Pooh behind him.
At the door he turned and said,
'Coming to see me have my bath?' "

The story of Chrisptoher Robin and Winnie the Pooh has been a constant source of amusement and delight to both children and adults since it was first conceived in 1924, and today there are few households that do not have one Winnie the Pooh book or artifact.

The original Winnie the Pooh bear was an Alpha Farnell, bought at Harrods in London as a first birthday present for A.A. Milne's son, Christopher Robin. At first Christopher simply called his companion "Bear" or "Teddy"

ABOVE Christopher Robin pictured with his father, A.A. Milne, and the original Winnie the Pooh Farnell bear.
LEFT Christopher Robin's toys (now quite worn), which became the subjects of A.A. Milne's famous books.
RIGHT A Christopher Robin doll, designed by the American bear artist R. John Wright.

(although he was known as "Edward Bear" by grownups). The name Winnie the Pooh only evolved later, when Christopher decided it was time his bear had a proper name. "Pooh" was the title Christopher gave to a swan he befriended during a stay at Decoy cottage in Arundel, Sussex, and "Winnie" was a North American bear Christopher had fallen in love with at London Zoo, that had once been the lucky mascot of the Canadian Brigade during the First World War. Milne's first collection of verse, *When We Were Very Young*, was published by Methuen in 1924, but although he wrote about a bear, it was not called Winnie the Pooh until December 1925, when Milne was drafting his second book,

and introduced Winnie the Pooh bumping down the stairs, trailing behind Christopher Robin. Ernest Shephard (who had illustrated Kenneth Grahame's *Wind in the Willows*) was commissioned to illustrate A.A. Milne's stories and poems, and his lovely drawings brought the characters alive. He based most of them on Christopher Robin's toy animals, but the model for Winnie the Pooh was primarily his son's Steiff teddy bear, called Growler. All the drawings were originally in black and white pencil, but in the 1970s, while in his nineties, Shephard was commissioned to add a color wash. The original pencil drawings can still be seen at the Victoria and Albert Museum in London.

FAR RIGHT The first American Winnie the Pooh toys were made by Agnes Brush in the 1940s. This bear was made for the F.A.O. Schwarz store in the 1950s.
CENTER RIGHT A British Merrythought novelty sleeping bag.
NEAR RIGHT This rather unusual looking flannel Winnie the Pooh was made by Gund in around 1950.

RIGHT Among the most collectible Winnie the Pooh toys are the wonderful limited edition characters produced by the famous American doll artist R. John Wright under license to Walt Disney. Shown here are his lovely Winnie the Pooh and Piglet.

With the exception of baby Roo, who, much to the anguish of Christopher Robin, was lost during an excursion to the apple orchard at Cotchford farm, Sussex (home of A.A. Milne and his family from 1925, and the setting for the Winnie the Pooh stories), the original toys—Pooh, Kanga, Piglet, Eeyore, and Tigger—have all survived, and are on display in the Central Children's Room at the Donnell Library Center in the New York Public Library in the United States.

It was not long before the commercial potential of Winnie the Pooh was recognized, and many manufacturers started to produce soft toy versions of A.A. Milne's lovable characters. The British Teddy Toy Company introduced a Winnie the Pooh series in the 1930s, and Chad Valley soon followed suit. Stephen Slesinger purchased the sole merchandising rights for Winnie the Pooh in the United States and Canada in 1929, but when Walt Disney took over the rights in 1960 Winnie the Pooh became a real phenomenon. The bear is also famous in Australia, and Joy Toys launched a line of Pooh characters in the 1960s. Winnie the Pooh and friends can be found on anything from pencil cases to sheets, handbags, and wallpaper. There are calendars, address books, diaries, journals, and of course, books. A.A. Milne's stories have been translated into over 20 languages, and there are few people in the world who have not at one time read a Winnie the Pooh book.

Bears on Paper

Paper provided a perfect canvas for the teddy bear, and it was not long before the teddy bear craze of the early 20th century hit postcards and greeting cards. Collecting cards and postcards is an excellent way of tracing changing styles and fashions, and in the case of portrait cards, may even help in dating a bear. Books featuring bears became very popular, and children's authors soon began to weave tales around the lovable new toy. Bears also hit the music scene, and sheet music for bear songs is collectible today. Bears were printed onto jigsaw puzzles and childhood games, and were made as cardboard cutouts that could be dressed in a variety of outfits. Bears also became the subject of the artist's brush. Watercolors and oil paintings both old and new have depicted the teddy bear and now adorn the walls of many an arctophile's home. The main consideration when buying any paper goods is condition. Torn or crumpled items will be far less desirable than pristine examples, and will only deteriorate further.

Postcards and cards

Postcards were introduced around the turn of the century, and soon numerous manufacturers were competing to produce the most appealing images. Sending a postcard was a quick and efficient way of communicating, and vast quantities were sent—so many that postcard collecting itself became a pastime. As methods of transportation improved, people traveled farther for their vacations, and the view cards that were produced also featured bears. The postcard boom coincided with the popularity of the teddy bear, so it is not surprising that bears were among the most common images on the cards. As printing methods became less expensive, cards became more commercial, and many were produced for more vulgar tastes (seaside cards are a perfect example.) Another type of card featuring bears was the portrait card, produced as an early type of photograph, and often depicting a child with a beautiful teddy bear.

ABOVE Prussian businessman Raphael Tuck introduced German printing methods to the production of cards and postcards in Britain in the 1860s. His embossed cards were so popular that he even supplied Queen Victoria. At this early stage the bears are shown as real ones, not teddies.
Height: $7^{1}/_{2}$in (19cm)
Approx value: $30–35 each

BELOW Seymour Eaton's popular Teddy Roosevelt bears appeared on a series of postcards in the U.S. in the early 20th century.
Height: 5$\frac{1}{2}$in (14cm) each
Approx value: $25-30 each

BELOW Teddy bears are particularly popular for childrens' birthday and Christmas cards. The card below is a typical example of those produced.
Height: 5$\frac{1}{2}$ in (14cm)
Approx value: $15-20

POST CARD

Mr. Robert Light
East Superior St.
Ottawa, Ill.

Loving Wishes for your 3rd. Birthday. Lots of wishes, love and kisses take their happy way, To some-one's little darling Who's three years old to-day.

ABOVE These two photographic postcards showing young children with their bears were published in Germany in around 1908. They show the typical sentimental poses that parents loved. It is interesting to note how large these two bears are. The cards have been hand-tinted with a color. This type of photographic card can be helpful when trying to date some old bears.
Height: 5$\frac{1}{2}$ in (14cm) each
Approx value: $20-25 each

ABOVE It can be rewarding to enhance your bear collection with postcards from all over the world. Shown here is an old Dutch card depicting a small child with a collection of toys.
Height: 3in (7.5cm)
Approx value: $18-20

Books

Early books depict the grizzly bear, but writers of children's stories soon adopted the teddy bear as their hero, using him in many guises to lead children through a whole range of adventures. Bears were particularly popular in British and American books, which were then translated into other languages. Famous literary bears include:

•Teddy B and Teddy G, by Seymour Eaton, 1905, U.S.

•Goldilocks and the Three Bears, c.1920, worldwide

•Rupert Bear, by Mary Tourtel, 1920, Britain

•Paddington Bear, by Michael Bond, 1958, Britain

•Winnie the Pooh, by A.A. Milne, 1924, Britain

•Blinky Bill, by Dorothy Wall, c.1935, Australia

Teddy bear books are popular among arctophiles and book collectors alike. They provide an interesting collecting area in their own right, because there is so much variety, and they have lavish illustrations. Sometimes pages from the original books have been taken out and put into albums, and although it is a pity that the books have been destroyed, the pages are still valuable. Any books in pristine condition, or that are first editions, will command a premium.

ABOVE Shown here is a selection of U.S. Golden & Wonder books about teddy bears dating from between 1926 and 1965. These books are so popular that they are still being reprinted today. However, first and second editions are most collectible, and those in pristine condition command a premium.
Height: 8in (20cm)
Approx value: $15-25 depending on edition and condition

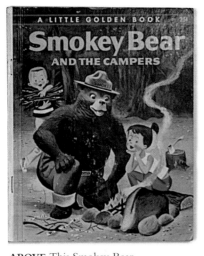

ABOVE This Smokey Bear book was published in the U.S. by Western Publishing Co, Inc. in 1961.
Height: 8in (20cm)
Approx value: $25-30

Goldenhair was asleep when the three bears came in. Said Big Bruin, "I'm hungry—to eat let's begin: [night, WHO HAS BEEN TO MY PORRIDGE!" he roared with such His voice was like wind down the chimney at night. "WHO HAS BEEN TO MY PORRIDGE!" growled out Mrs. Her voice was like cats fighting up in a tree. [B— "WHO HAS BEEN TO MY PORRIDGE, AND EATEN IT ALL!" Young Tiny-cub said in a voice very small.

"WHO HAS BEEN SITTING IN MY GREAT ARM-CHAIR!" In a voice like a thunder-storm roared the big bear. "WHO HAS BEEN SITTING IN MY GOOD ARM-CHAIR!" Growled out Mammy Muff like a sow in despair. "WHO HAS SAT IN MY NICE CHAIR, AND BROKEN IT DOWN!" Young Tiny-cub said, and so fierce was his frown, That his mother said, with pride to his father said, "There! See our pet Tiny-cub can look just like a bear."

LEFT The story of *Goldilocks and The Three Bears* is believed to be the oldest children's bear story, although its origins are unknown, because early versions exist in almost every language. This page has been taken from a very early edition and pasted into a scrap book.
Height: 10¼in (26cm)
Approx value: $25-30

RIGHT U.S. author, Seymour Eaton (real name Paul Piper), created the Roosevelt Bears, Teddy B and Teddy G, in 1905. The stories were initially published as a series in twenty leading newspapers before being published in book form. The two bears resemble grizzly bears rather than the later teddy bear, and it was not until Eaton's second volume, *More About Teddy B and Teddy G, The Roosevelt Bears*, that he called his bears "teddy bears." The first volume, *The Roosevelt Bears—Their Travels and Adventures*, was illustrated by Floyd Campbell, but the next two were illustrated by R.K. Culver, and the last one by Francis P. Wightman and William K. Sweeney. These four books are highly collectible, and a whole set is very rare and highly prized. The Roosevelt bears were so

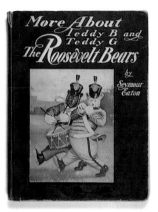
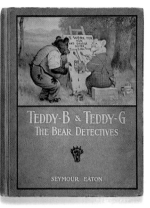

popular with children that soon they appeared on postcards, chinaware, and board games in the United States. Teddy B and Teddy G outfits were also made for children's own teddy bears (*see p.98*). Shown above are volumes one, two, and four of the Roosevelt books with a selection of the inside pages (*see right*).
Height: 11in (28cm)
Approx value: $225-350

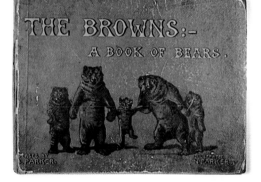

ABOVE AND ABOVE RIGHT
The Browns—A Book of Bears was published in Edinburgh and London by W. and R. Chambers in 1906. It consists of twelve verses written by B. Parker illustrated with grizzly bears drawn by N. Parker.
Height: 13in (33cm)
Approx value: $200 plus

RIGHT Cut-out dolls with paper outfits were very popular. This bear comes with five separate outfits. The set was published around 1910 by J. Ottmann Litho. Co. in New York and is still in its original envelope, which makes it particularly collectible.
Height: 6in (15cm)
Approx value: $350 plus

Sheet music

As soon as teddy bears became popular, they entered into the world of song. It is estimated that between 1907 and 1911 more than 40 songs had the name "teddy bear" in the title. Perhaps the most popular teddy tune is *The Teddy Bears Picnic*, written by American composer, John W. Bratton in 1907, and made popular with British children in the 1930s when songwriter Jimmy Kennedy put the words to music. Other sheet music that appears on the market includes the *Sack Waltz* published around 1906 by the Deluxe Music Company, and *Teddy Bear Pieces* by J.S. Fearis, published by McKinley Music in the United States around 1907. Examples in pristine condition will command a premium, as will any signed copies or first editions.

Paintings

Beautiful paintings of bears, either on their own or with young children, have a lasting appeal. Bears have been reproduced in oils, pastels, and watercolors, and in a variety of contexts. One of the most popular British watercolorists is Leigh Beavis West, and her classical portraits of teddy bears have been reproduced many times on stationery and gift products, and appear in many private collections, not only in Britain, but throughout the world.

ABOVE AND LEFT This selection of sheet music represents only a few of the teddy bear pieces written in the early 20th century. Such a variety means it is possible to build up quite a collection.
Height: 11–13in (23–34cm)
Approx value: $45–50 plus

RIGHT Leigh Beavis West's "Bear and Bumble" captures the charm of the teddy bear. Painted in gouache, it has been signed, mounted, and framed.
Height: 14in (36.4cm)
Approx value: $950–1,200

RIGHT British collector and painter Ray Campbell often uses teddy bears as his subjects for his oil paintings. Shown here is "Good Friends".
Height: 19in (48cm)
Approx value: $800–1,000

Postage stamps

Bear loving philatelists are surprisingly well-catered to, and at a relatively low price. Throughout the world bears have appeared on stamps, from Poland and Russia to the United States. The bears in the stamps vary from black bears and polar bears to teddy bears and literary bears. Because special edition stamps are always being issued, stamps with bears on them can provide an easily obtainable addition to your bear collection. First editions are particularly collectible.

BELOW This puzzle from around 1984 is one of a series based on the illustrations in a book by Michael Hague called *Alphabears*. The fact that no pieces are missing from this one will add to its value.
Height: 7in (18cm)
Approx value: $5

RIGHT This very rare Teddy Roosevelt card game consists of 95 cards showing Teddy Roosevelt on a hunting trip. It was made by The Teddy Bear Novelty Company in New York in around 1907.
Height: 3$\frac{1}{2}$in (9cm) each card
Approx value: $500 plus

ABOVE AND RIGHT In Britain the Royal Mail issued a series of colorful Greetings Book stamps in 1989, 1990, 1993, and 1994 featuring the literary characters, Rupert Bear, The Three Bears, and Paddington. The four stamps shown above represent a selection of the images that appeared on the stamps. Other stamps include images of Beatrix Potter's Peter Rabbit, and further images of Rupert Bear and Paddington.
Height: 1in
Approx value: $2 upwards

Games and puzzles

Toys, games and puzzles featuring teddy bears have been made over a long period of time, from the beginning of the 20th century to the present day. They can be found at the various toy fairs around the world, but lucky discoveries can also be made at tag sales and flea markets. Old examples are particularly desirable, especially if they are in good condition, but relatively recent games are also eagerly sought after. Condition will affect the price, particularly if, as in the case of jigsaw puzzles, there are pieces missing. Do check before you buy a puzzle, as it can be very disappointing to get your purchase home and find a vital piece is missing. Other teddy bear games and toys that appear on the market include card games and board games.

Bears in Other Media

Teddy bears have been made in virtually every medium, and bears in other media can be an inexpensive way of adding to any bear collection. Bears were popular before the teddy bear craze of 1905, and many items made before this time, such as the Black Forest wooden bears shown on this page, resemble true bears rather than the teddy bear of Clifford Berryman's cartoons. During the early years of teddy bear mania manufacturers recognized the great commercial potential of bears and started to incorporate them into an even larger variety of products. Porcelain and china (often low-quality and mass-produced) abound with paintings of bears in many poses. Modern jewelry, such as pins and earrings, can be bought in the shape of bears, and old silver novelties, made mainly in Birmingham, England, provide another interesting collecting area. Be careful when buying what you think is an antique, because many modern-day reproductions can easily be mistaken for originals.

Wooden bears

A number of beautifully carved wooden bears were produced at the end of the 19th century. Known as Black Forest bears, many were in fact made in Switzerland (not Germany). Many of these carved bears are connected with smoking—ashtrays, matchbox holders, pipe holders, and smoker's tables were all produced with bears incorporated into them. Others are desk or dressing table accessories—often bears appear on the back of hair brushes and clothes brushes. Some were sold as souvenirs and may be engraved. Modern reproductions have also been made, and it is important to be aware of this—unfortunately only experience can tell you how to spot the difference, and you may need to enlist the help of a specialist if in doubt.

LEFT The wooden bear ashtray and matchbox holder on the far left represent just some of the numerous wooden smokers' accessories that appear on the market. Many other Black Forest bears were simply ornamental—the bear on the near left is a typical example. Other bears were incorporated into wooden trays.
Height: 4 to 6in (10 to 15cm)
Approx value: $125–175 each

RIGHT This very large bear from around 1890 displays exceptionally high-quality carving—the nose, teeth, and tongue are all clearly defined. This particular carving is very unusual, but similar examples, made as umbrella stands, are more popular.
Height: 43in (109cm) to the top of the staff
Approx value: $1,700

Silver and metal

Bears were used to decorate a variety of objects, from sophisticated hat pins to baby rattles, button hooks, and condiment sets. Many of them were produced in Birmingham, England, and the British hallmarking system has made it easy to date these things precisely, because all silver should have the maker's mark and date stamped on it. Modern examples are also collectible, although they should not be mistaken for antiques.

China

Chinaware featuring teddy bears was often produced for children, either in the form of dolls' tea services or as cups, plates, and bowls for the children themselves. Many other items were made as ornaments. Most of the china was made in England and Germany. Much of it was mass-produced and is usually unmarked. Any pieces by a top manufacturer will be particularly valuable, especially if in good condition.

ABOVE This pepper shaker was made in Birmingham in 1910. The bear's head lifts off to allow for refilling.
Height: 2in (5cm)
Approx value: $235

ABOVE When this American metal teddy bear chime from 1907 is moved along, the bear dances and rings the bells.
Height: 7in (18cm)
Approx value: $1,250

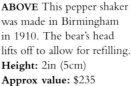

LEFT The English china decorator, Jean Allen, hand-painted a variety of plates from the 1930s to the 1950s, featuring gollies and bears; these are highly collectible today. They are all one-of-a-kinds, and she does not even use plates from the same factory.
Size: 12in (30.5cm) diameter
Approx value: $550

LEFT Bretby Art Pottery in Derbyshire, England, made this earthenware umbrella stand around 1885. Although stands were made with other animals incorporated into them, those with bears on are very rare and highly sought after.
Height: 25in (xcm)
Approx value: $1,500

ABOVE This bear with a dog is one of a series of highly collectible miniature porcelain figures with crocheted clothes made in Germany around 1910.
Height: 2in (5cm)
Approx value: $350

ABOVE These German bisque bears from around 1900 are particularly desirable because they are in excellent condition and are still a complete set.
Height: 5in (13cm) down
Approx value: $400 the set

Novelties

Ever since teddy bears were first made, manufacturers have produced novelties. The earliest bears often had a growler or squeaking mechanism, but it was not long before designers conjured up more exciting things for their bears to do. Musical bears were made in Germany, and Steiff and Bing are particularly famous for their mechanical bears that walked, danced, or tumbled. In America, the "Electric Eye" bear had eyes that lit up, and Strauss made a whistling teddy. Bears were also incorporated into other products. There were bear bags, purses, nightdress cases, and hand muffs. A lot of these items were made for young children, and many, such as a children's gas mask, were produced during the Second World War to take away some of the terror of war. The nursery was another popular area for teddy bear things—bears were made to conceal hot water bottles or babies' milk bottles, while others were made into rattles. Although the major manufacturers, such as Steiff in Germany, and Merrythought in England, produced novelty items, there are many other novelties whose makers cannot be identified—some of them were even made by hand.

RIGHT The mechanism that works this bear on a stick is very simple. When the wooden block is pushed up the stick, the bear does a handstand over the top. Made in Germany by an unknown maker around 1915, the bear has gold bristle mohair and black button eyes. He has an unjointed neck and wire jointing through his arms. He is attached to the stick by wire, and his hands are stitched together with cotton.
Height: 20in (51cm) with stick
Approx value: $125-185

ABOVE Tumbling bears seem to hold a particular attraction for collectors. Steiff produced the tumbling teddy somersaulting over the top of this page in 1908. The arms are used as a key, which, when wound backwards, cause the bear to tumble forwards. Other tumbling animals were produced by Steiff, including a monkey, elephant, clown, and Eskimo. Bing also made mechanical bears (*see pp.38-9*). The Steiff tumbling bear was made in light brown, dark brown, or white mohair. The bears can be found in working order, but any that have broken are very difficult to repair.
Height: 14in (35.5cm)
Approx value: $2,500

BELOW Several unidentified manufacturers produced bears in the form of purses. These well-loved items are often quite worn, but are popular because of their nostalgic appeal. This one has all the typical features of a standard early bear—black shoe-button eyes, black stitched nose, swivel head, and fully-jointed limbs.
Height: 16in (40.6cm)
Approx value $800 plus

BELOW This teddy bear gas mask is a typical example of those produced during the Second World War to soften the horror of war for children. The bear has been sewn onto the case. He is made of cotton plush and filled with kapok. It is not surprising that few of these survived the war.
Height: 12in (30.5cm)
Approx value: $100-125

BELOW Merrythought produced this hand muff in the 1960s. Made of gold mohair, the bear has the typical smiling face of the Cheeky bear (*see pp.70-71*). Other Merrythought novelties include sleeping bags incorporating many different animals, among them Walt Disney characters.
Height: 15in (38cm)
Approx value: $550

ABOVE The fact that this bear purse is accompanied by a picture of it with its original owner will add to its value.
Height: 16in (40.6cm)
Approx value: $800 plus

ABOVE The uncertain quality of this Dorothy bag suggests it was handmade, probably in England, around 1916. The bag and the bear's head are both mohair.
Height: 12in (30.5cm)
Approx value: $80-120

A Bear Lover's Guide

Care, Repair, and Restoration

When you buy an old bear he will inevitably need some care and attention, and just as you would not neglect an antique table you had bought, so you must not neglect your bear. Simple repairs can be done at home, but anything more complicated should be undertaken by a professional restorer. These are listed in the numerous teddy bear magazines published worldwide, or your local teddy bear store will be able to advise you. When you take your bear to be restored it is very important to make it clear to the restorer how you want your bear to look, and which of his original features you don't want to be touched, so that he still retains his old charm when he comes back to you.

RIGHT AND LEFT
The large blond Steiff on the left needs heavy restoration. He has been given a pair of children's socks to keep the stuffing in his feet. His nose is very fragile—a common problem caused by too much kissing. His little Farnell friend is also badly in need of some attention. The bear on the right needs his pads restored and his ears have been put on wrong.

AWAITING RESTORATION
Before having your bear restored it is important to consider whether it will be successful—sometimes a bear may be in such a bad state that putting him back together again may not only be very expensive but may also yield disappointing results. Bears like the Steiff and Farnell shown here are good examples of ones that should be professionally restored, because they are both valuable collector's items, and money spent on them will only increase their value. In addition, the fabric is of such high quality that it will respond well to sympathetic restoration, whereas fabric of lesser quality may disintegrate. However, if your bear is an old cherished friend, even though the cost of restoration may exceed its value, you may still prefer to have the repairs done rather than lose the bear forever.

LEFT This bear is in a sorry state. He has had his pads restored incorrectly and they do not follow the line of the originals. Also, the wrong type of material has been used, and it is clearly not the color it should be. He has worn extremely thin and restoration may be difficult.

RIGHT This bear is in very poor condition. His fabric has lost all its pile and is very fragile. His missing ear could be restored by splitting the existing one into two and backing both with new material. His eyes need replacing because he has lost one of the originals. Because he is of poor-quality mohair, any restoration will not be perfect.

LEFT These two bears are known as Marjorie's bears after the little girl who owned them around 1915. They are quite simple bears made of bristle mohair and were clearly restored and dressed a long time ago.

BADLY RESTORED

Old bears have often suffered a great deal of wear and tear because of the love and affection they have had bestowed on them by their childhood owners. They lose limbs, have ears and noses pulled out, and may have lost their stitching. Obviously, mothers were frequently called upon to mend the bears, and the repairs were often carried out unsympathetically, using any materials on hand—the wrong type and color of thread, odd glass eyes, and paw pads made from all sorts of materials. Luckily, these things can all be restored correctly with a little hard work. Nowadays, with the greater awareness of old bears and the increasing number of books that are available about them, it is possible to get advice about how your bear should be restored, or to look him up in a good bear book, identify and date him, and see how he should look like before commissioning any repairs.

DIFFICULT TO RESTORE

Some bears are in very bad condition and may be difficult to restore satisfactorily. The greatest problem is very dry, brittle fabric. This can be hard for the restorer to work with because it is often rotten and will crumble away when it is stitched. Sometimes old bears have been repaired with glue, and again this can be very difficult to remove. If the material is weak around the muzzle and a nose needs replacing it is possible to find a matching-color mohair and set in a new muzzle which will hold together when stitching back the nose and mouth. Obviously the new seams will be visible around the muzzle, but this is preferable to having a bear with a deteriorating muzzle and no nose and mouth at all. Small holes in the body and the pads can be patched up in a similar way, and if the mohair is otherwise still quite good, the patches will not be visible. However, if a bear is very worn all over, you can't do anything about it—he can't have a hair transplant!

SHOULD NOT BE RESTORED

There are some bears that cannot be restored without altering the original character. This is particularly true of bears that were repaired by their first owner a long time ago, and that may have odd eyes or strange fabric, or may have had a crooked nose sewn on lovingly by a small child. All these things are part of the bear's family history, and if they are changed it may drastically change the character of the bear. Marjorie's bears shown here are typical examples of bears that should not be altered. The bear on the right of the picture has eyes that are far too large for her, giving her a rather surprised expression, and her friend's eyes don't match. But although the bears look odd, their features complement their old-fashioned clothes and accessories and it would be a shame to change them. It is really important if you have a bear you love but that is not quite right, to be very explicit to the restorer as to what you want retained—otherwise you may find the feature you loved most about your bear is now missing!

MATERIALS AND STUFFING

If a bear needs patching you should try and use new materials as close to the original in color and texture as possible; these are available through suppliers throughout the world and are listed in teddy bear directories. The stuffing in old bears can need replenishing or replacing completely, and kapok and wood wool are still available for this purpose. Noses and claws should be replaced using embroidery silk, matching the color as near to the original as you can. If the nose looks a bit shiny, dip your finger in some vacuum cleaner dust and rub the nose to dull it, or add a dusting of talcum powder. A large variety of new glass eyes is available that are very close to the originals. It is a good idea to look at fairs and garage sales for old mohair stuffed toys in poor condition, because these can be dismantled to repair old bears.

wood wool   kapok

The restorer is carefully undoing the stitching on the bear so that she can replenish his limp stuffing.

Once the bear has been restuffed, it is important to hand-sew the center seam very neatly using a matching yarn.

A variety of mohair and felts useful in restoring your bear

A tilt growler, *left*, and two old squeakers, *above*

RIGHT When this c.1908 center-seam Steiff was recently bought by its owner she discovered that its stuffing had almost reduced to powder. He also needs new nose stitching and a new smile, and his pads need some attention. However, his coat is in good condition, and he will benefit from restoration. When restuffing a bear it is important to remember that this may alter the angle of the head. Sometimes a slight droop can be very attractive (pre-Second World War Chilterns were deliberately made with a tilting head), so make sure your bear is not stuffed too tightly.

BEFORE

EYES

Old bears are often missing one or both eyes, or they may have replacement eyes that may make them look ridiculous. If just one eye is missing it is very difficult to find a matching one. Usually the only solution is to buy a new pair. But do not throw the original one away beccause you never know, you might find one to match it one day. The earliest bears had black boot-button eyes, and these are in fact the ones least likely to be missing today, and even if they are, it is easy to find replacements. Glass eyes were often attached to a length of wire and tied to the back of the bear's head. Many anxious parents removed these before giving the bear to a child, and replaced them with any number of things, from old plastic buttons to bits of felt. Sometimes wool has even been stitched over the socket to simulate an eye, giving the bear a very strange appearance. Both amber and black, and clear glass eyes can be purchased today. However, it is essential to take your bear with you when buying his eyes, so that you can try them against his face. If they are too big, your bear is in danger of looking like a goldfish!

It is possible to replace your bear's eyes yourself. Remove the old eyes with pliers. It is important to have a long needle, because the thread needs to be pulled through to the back of the head and tied into a knot at the back.

BELOW The saggy blond mohair Steiff on the left has been transformed into the beautiful bear shown here. He has been cleaned, his stuffing has been replaced, and his nose and mouth stitching have been resewn. His replacement paw pads have been removed and new ones added.

The restorer is removing the one remaining ear of this bear so that she can dismantle it to make two new ones.

Before restitching, make sure there is no old thread attached. Try to copy the design of the original nose as far as possible.

AFTER

NOSE AND EARS

The muzzle is one of the most vulnerable areas on vintage bears, and sometimes the only solution to a worn one is to cover the whole muzzle with new fabric and sew on a new nose and mouth. Wherever possible, try and use old mohair that matches the original. Sometimes you can use the reverse of the material to obtain a more authentic shaved look. Ears are difficult to replace if they are completely missing, because it will be difficult to find a mohair that matches exactly in color and texture, and your bear may look odd. If one ear is present it is easier, because the one ear can be divided into two and a new one made.

For the positioning of the ears look at old photographs and books. Remember that there is a limit to what the restorer can do, and any restoration on the face is particularly difficult to disguise.

JOINTS

The cardboard disks used for jointed bears are secured with metal washers, cotter pins, and nails, and you may find that these have rusted. Sometimes the nails have rusted so much that it is impossible to pull them out, and when this happens the only solution is to snap them off. This is one reason why you should never immerse your bear in water, not even modern examples, because these also have metal pins. Some of the earlier bears had metal joints rather than cardboard ones, and these may have eaten into the material and need replacing with new joints. Old cardboard joints may also need replacing because they often disintegrate. New joints, washers, and pins can all be bought from a toy or bear supplier.

PADS

Unfortunately it is very rare to find an old bear with all its original pads, but you may be lucky and discover that when you remove the replacement pads the bear still has some of the originals underneath. If the pads are still present but have holes in them, you can insert felt carefully behind the hole and use small over-stitches to secure the patch. Always keep the original label, and sew it back onto the pad afterward. To re-create rexine, which is no longer available, use woven cotton painted with acrylic paint.

The restorer is undoing an old cotter pin with pliers so that she can remove the disintegrated arm joint and replace it with a new hard-board joint and pin.

To reach the neck joint unstitch the center seam and remove some of the stuffing. Undo the cotter pin so that the head can be removed and a new joint put in place.

Place a new piece of felt on the pad and cut around it to fit

Pin the cut piece of felt to the pad before sewing it in place

BEFORE

LEFT At first glance it is difficult to recognize that this sorry sight is even a bear. He arrived with his ears by his side, looking completely forlorn. His mohair coat is very dirty, and his stuffing is loose in his arm. The mohair on his muzzle is virtually threadbare, and the mouth and nose stitching have almost disappeared. His paw pads need new stitching, and his pads need replacing. At the moment he has a sock on his foot to keep his stuffing from falling out.

BEFORE

AFTER

WASHING AND CLEANING

Before washing your bear inspect his coat carefully for bugs, and then either brush him or vacuum him with a nozzle covered with thin cloth to remove any loose dust. Sit the bear on a towel and fill a bowl with cool water. Add a gentle wool wash to the water and work up a lather (detergent or shampoo can be too soapy and will be difficult to rinse off). Using a small brush—a soft toothbrush is ideal—work the foam into the fur making sure you don't get the

fabric too wet. When you have covered the whole surface, remove as much of the foam as you can with a dry cloth, then remove the rest with a damp cloth. Keep rinsing out the cloth in the water and make sure that you have gotten all the soap out—if any is left, the mohair will be sticky when it is dry and attract dirt. Let your bear dry naturally rather than using a hair dryer; putting him in an open cupboard is an ideal solution. When his fur is dry use a fine metal comb to fluff it up.

AFTER

RIGHT It is hard to believe that this bear is the same as the one on the left. He has been transformed: his muzzle has been reinforced with mohair and a new nose and mouth stitched onto it; his pads have been replaced and his claws re-stitched; and he has been cleaned and his stuffing replaced.

HANDY HINTS

•Wash very dirty bears more than once to get them clean—the results are worth it

•Inspect old bears regularly for moths

•Brush your bear with a soft brush to keep him dustfree, because dirt and dust attract insects

•Once a year wipe the bears in your collection with a damp cloth wrung out in clear water. Allow the bears to dry and then comb them through

•Do not sit your bear in direct sunlight because sunlight will cause him to fade

•Placing the bear near central heating or smoke of any kind will discolor him

•Do not wrap the bear in plastic because it will cause him to rot

•Put very dirty bears in a plastic bag of dry oatmeal to draw out the grime. Then wash the bear if it is still dirty

Dressed Bears

There has always been a fascination with dressing up, whether it is ourselves or our dolls and bears. Ever since the first teddy bear was made at the beginning of the 20th century, bears have been dressed in fine and elaborate clothes, and even those that were not originally dressed, often now wear outfits carefully chosen or made by their loving owners. For many collectors dressing a bear adds to its character, but others think it is unnecessary and believe, for example, that a beautiful old Steiff would be spoiled by covering it up. For those who like dressed bears there is a great variety on the market, but remember, before buying a dressed bear, look under his clothes—you don't want to get home and find he has an arm missing!

LEFT This 1950s bear was dressed in top hat and tails for his owner's wedding. Unfortunately, some time after the honeymoon he was quite badly mauled by a dog, and now he has a leg, one ear, and an eye missing. Dressing him in a pirate's costume has cleverly concealed all his injuries and given the bear a character of his own. Who would know that there is no eye under his patch?

RIGHT Valentina, a 1910 bear by an unidentified maker, is dressed in old family clothes that will continue to protect her mohair coat—which is still in good condition—from any further wear.

Bears dressed for protection

Many new owners dress their recently acquired vintage bears to protect them from further wear and tear. If a bear is going bald it can become very fragile and even disintegrate, and covering it up with clothes will help to prolong its life. Often in the past old lisle stockings have been put over paw pads to prevent the bear's stuffing from falling out. The clothes people choose vary greatly. Good seamstresses may want to make their bears' outfits themselves, but many others may prefer to maintain the period of their bear and try and find Victorian and Edwardian children's clothes that with a little alteration will fit. Otherwise, you can order clothes from one of the bear clothiers advertised in bear magazines.

Three 1935 Eduard Crämer Bearkins modeling their clothes

Penny Chalmer's bears   "Augustus"

Factory-dressed bears

Vintage bears in their original clothing are rare, particularly the very early ones. One of the first dressed bears was the Ally Bear made by the British firm of Harwin and Co. (*see p. 78*). Chiltern's first bear, Master Teddy, was also dressed (*see p. 72*), as were the mechanical bears of Schuco and Bing in Germany. Many have clothes that cannot be removed, but one German firm, Eduard Cramer (*see p. 50*), made a Bearkins for the U.S. department store F.A.O. Schwarz that came with a suitcase and changes of clothes. Dressing bears was very popular after the Second World War when mohair was expensive—both Schuco and Steiff in Germany dressed their bears at this time, as did Merrythought in Britain.

Recently-dressed bears

Many collectors like to dress their bears in a full outfit while others just add a simple accessory, such as an antique lace collar, a bow tie, or old spectacles. By shopping around at flea markets you can find some very good bargains. Augustus, shown here, an unidentified bear from around 1912, is a typical example of a bear recently dressed by his owner. He is wearing a velvet waistcoat made specially for him and an antique shirt collar To complete the outfit he has an old fob watch. Other recently-dressed bears are those made by modern bear artists, who often use antique clothing. The two bears on the far left were made by British bear artist Penny Chalmers (*see p. 134*), who uses antique lace and velvets.

Bears dressed by their original owners

Sometimes a collector is lucky enough to discover a bear that has been dressed by its original owner. You can find out the age of the clothes your bear is wearing if he is accompanied by old family pictures of him with his outfit, or by looking at the materials used, but remember that some bears have been dressed recently in old clothes. It was very popular after the First World War to cut up old military uniforms that were no longer needed and dress family bears up as soldiers. Johnny Bear shown on the far left is a typical example. Other bears from this time were dressed in old dolls' clothes. The little bear seen on the near left dates from around 1915. She is wearing hand-knitted dolls' clothes and is sitting on a Victorian dolls' house chair.

Display and Storage

When you start adding to your bear collection you can easily run out of space, so a little careful planning is necessary. The most important consideration with any bear, old or new, is to make sure it is not kept in direct sunlight, because it will fade. Many people like to display their bears in a glass-fronted display cabinet, and these can be custom-built to suit individual requirements. Other collectors don't like the idea of their bears being locked away and prefer having them sit around as part of the family on shelves, children's high chairs, or tables that can be picked up for a relatively low cost at antiques sales. Alternatively, a few simple shelves could be built to house your bears. Bears look attractive diplayed with interesting props, and miniature bears especially need something to support them.

Wherever you put your old bears, it is important that they are not placed where they will be handled too much, because they will become worn, and you should be particularly careful if you have dogs: many bears end up in bear hospitals with savage wounds.

LEFT This old German children's rocking horse from around 1880 provides the perfect solution for displaying a number of bears together in one place. Other interesting props include baby carriages and nursery furniture. Teddy bears also enjoy sitting on high chairs that keep them out of the way of threatening dogs. **Height:** 30in (76cm)

Miniature bears

Miniature bears have special problems when it comes to display because they are so tiny they can easily get lost or become hidden if on a shelf cluttered with other things. The best way of viewing small bears is at eye level, so a glass cabinet or wall shelves can be ideal. They can also look charming when put with miniature dolls' house furniture—chairs, tables, desks, and even miniature baby carriages and cribs provide endless possibilities for smaller bears. Victorian glass domes available from antiques stores are another way of displaying small bears in an attractive way.

Larger bears

Do remember when buying large bears that you need some-where to sit them—often they are too big to fit in glass cabinets or to sit on shelves. Particularly large bears can sit on household chairs quite happily. They also like playing in children's cars and sleighs. For more standard size bears, nursery furniture can be suitable, and baby carriages look wonderful when filled with bears. Old high chairs and rock-ing horses are also worth looking for.

Props

Hunting for props for your teddy bears can provide endless fun, and can become as much of a hobby as collecting the bears themselves. Items such as suitcases, drums, and colored balls can be bought from antiques fairs and garage sales, but you may find that you have many things stored away from your childhood that your bears would like to play with. Accessories can also add to the appearance of your bear—fob watches and old spectacles are just some suggestions.

ABOVE LEFT AND RIGHT
The tiny bears above are sitting at a wooden desk taken from a dolls' house; the ones on the right are enjoying a ride in a small wicker sleigh.
Height: *desk* 4in (10cm); *sleigh* 4in (10cm)

RIGHT Bears look attractive sitting on dolls' chairs like the Victorian one shown here. The 1950s drums below are another handy prop.
Height: *chair* 18in (46cm); *drums* 6in (15cm)

BELOW This 1930s metal train can provide a useful seat for a number of bears.
Length: 24in (61cm)

Storage

In the past, bears stored in attics have suffered a lot of damage because of dampness and extremes of temper-ature. Bears need to be stored in a cool, dry place in a cardboard box (a cotton pillow case is an alternative) with acid-free tissue paper. Lavender bags, cedar balls, or moth balls should be packed with the bears to stop moths and insects eating them. Never store bears in plastic bags because this will cause mold.

Glossary

ANNIVERSARY BEAR A teddy bear made by a long-established manufacturer to mark an important date.

ART SILK PLUSH (Artificial silk plush) An artificial fiber produced from wood or cotton, used for teddy bears from the 1930s onward.

ARTIST BEAR A bear designed and made by an individual, sometimes with the help of others, and finished by hand.

BAT-WING NOSE A distinctive type of stitching made to resemble bat wings.

BOOT-BUTTON EYES Black wooden eyes with metal loops on the back, very similar in appearance to old boot-buttons. Particularly popular for the earliest teddy bears.

BURLAP Coarse, heavy fabric woven from jute or hemp, used for some early stuffed toys. Also known as hessian.

CELLULOID An artificial material produced from pyroxylin, a type of cellulose, and camphor.

CLIPPED MOHAIR Mohair cut short, usually on the muzzle or the tops of the feet.

COTTON PLUSH An inexpensive material woven from cotton, used on bears around the time of the Second World War.

COTTON WASTE/COTTON SUB
See Substitute.

DISTRESSED MOHAIR Mohair plush made to look antique, particularly popular among bear artists and manufacturers producing replicas.

DUAL PLUSH Mohair that has had its ends painted with a second color. Also known as tipped mohair.

EXCELSIOR/WOOD WOOL A soft mixture of long, thin wood shavings used for stuffing.

FOOT PADS The bottom of the feet, usually made of felt or rexine, but also leather.

GOO GOO EYES/ GOOGLY EYES Distinctively large, round, often movable eyes that glance to the side.

GROWLER The voice box that produces a growl or roar.

HUMP A pronounced lump on the back of the bear, introduced by Steiff, but copied by many other manufacturers in the early 20th century.

INSET MUZZLE A muzzle made of a separate piece of material sewn into the face.

JOINTED Bears with movable arms, legs, and heads.

KAPOK A silky lightweight fiber derived from a seed pod and used for stuffing.

LATEX A natural material used to produce rubber.

LIMITED EDITION Teddy bears produced in a limited number, making them particularly collectible.

MOHAIR PLUSH Originally a plush made from the fleece of a Turkish angora goat, but today more likely to be a mixture of wool and cotton.

MUZZLE A protruding snout.

PAW PADS The pads at the end of the "arms."

PLUSH A fabric with a cut pile that is longer and softer than velvet.

REPLICA A direct copy of an antique teddy bear, produced by the original manufacturer, often using old factory patterns, and usually in a limited number.

REXINE Shiny leather cloth or oilskin used for paw pads, mainly on English bears after the Second World War. Often the coating has worn off leaving the cotton backing.

ROD BEAR A type of bear introduced by Steiff with metal rodded joints that run through the body

SEALING WAX A wax produced to seal documents, used in the early 20th century to make realistically molded noses for teddy bears.

STICK BEAR A small, inexpensive type of bear, often unjointed, made in vast quantities in the U.S.

SUBSTITUTE/"SUB-WASTE" Waste left over from the manufacture of cotton in factories, introduced as a stuffing mainly for British teddy bears after the First World War when other materials became difficult to obtain.

SWING TAG A paper identification tag attached to a bear and printed with the manufacturer's details.

TIPPED *See Dual Plush*

ULTRASUEDE A synthetic suede-looking material introduced in the U.S. and used for paw pads.

WEBBED CLAW STITCHING Claw stitching, used particularly by Merrythought and Farnell, which resembles webbing.

WOOD WOOL *See Excelsior*

YES/NO A type of teddy bear produced by the German manufacturer, Schuco; by moving the tail the head can be turned left to right or up and down.

ZOTTY BEAR A long-haired teddy bear with an open mouth introduced by Steiff, but later copied by a number of other manufacturers.

Gazetteer

TEDDY BEAR ARTISTS

Details of artists
featured in this book:

Australia

Heather Brooks
Bearly Collectable
P O Box 89, Mittagong
N.S.W. 2575

Lexie Haworth
The Bears of Haworth Cottage
7 Walsh Crescent
North Nowra
N.S.W. 2541

Roasalie Macleman
Macbears
R.S.D. T15
Woodstock-on-Loddon
Victoria 3539

Briony Nottage
House of Brook Bri
451 Henley Beach Road
Lockleys
South Australia 3052

Deborah Sargentson
Nostalgia Bears
44 Ivanhoe Grove
Chadstone, Victoria 3148

Austria

Karin Kronsteiner
Karin Kronsteiner's
Künstlerbären
Krenngasse
A-8010 Graz

Belgium

Jean Van Meeuwe Slater
Just For You
Mereldreef 119
B3140
Keerbergen

Canada

Hana Franklin
25 Rivercourt Blvd.
Toronto
Ontario
M4J 3A3

Cherie Friendship
Friendship Teddy Bear Factory
21 Ridgevale Drive
Makham
Ontario
L3P 3J2

Lesley Mallet
Fred Bears
154 Cambridge Court
Richmond Hill
Ontario
L4C 6E7

Joan Rankin
155 Hochelaga St. W.
Moose Jaw, SK
S6H 2G2

England

Penny Chalmers
The Bear's Den
80 The Street
West Horley
Surrey KT22 6BE

Jo Greeno
9 Cranley Close
Guildford
Surrey GU1 2JN

Gregory Gyllenship
109 Bow Road
London E3 2AN

Nicola Perkins
Tree Top Bears
2 The Spinney
Madeley Heath, Nr Crewe
Cheshire CW3 9TB

Jennie Sharman-Cox
Mister Bear
17 Lord Roberts Avenue
Leigh-on-Sea
Essex SS9 1ND

Stacey Lee Terry
Bo Bears
25 Hillcrest Way
Buckingham MK18 1HJ

Frank Webster
Charnwood Bears
4 Ashby Square
Loughborough
Leics. LE11 0AA

France

Aline Cousin
Boite 7082
70 rue du Docteur Sureau
93160 Noisy Le Grand

Marcelle Goffin
34 rue Lieu de Santé
76000 Rouen

Marylou Jouet
1 rue Emile Bernard
35700 Rennes

Germany

Verena Greene-Christ
Teddies by Vera & Verena
Schulstrasse 25
D-56479 Neunkirchen/WW

Ineke Weber
Ineke's Teddybären
Robienstrasse 61
D-80935 Munich

Heidrun Winkler-Lamann
Drüne Bären
Rheinlandstrasse 26
D-65824 Schwalbach

Ireland

Joan Hanna
Craft T Bears
Mount Windsor
Farnahoe
Innishannon
Co. Cork

Japan

Michi and Hiro Takahashi
Fairy Chuckle
301-5-27-31
Higashifuchinobe
Sagamihara-shi
Kanagawa 229

Miyuki Wada
Miyuki Bears
2-3 Nangu-Cho
Ashiya-City Hyogo 659

Mayumi Watanabe
Mammie Bears
2-11-20 Shoan
Suginami-ku
Tokyo 167

The Netherlands

Jane Humme
Oud Boegraafsweg 95
2411 HX Bodegraven

Annemieke Koetse
Beofje Bears
Willam de Zweijgerlaan 8
2012 SC
Haarlem

New Zealand

Janis Harris
Almost South Pole
23 Pohutukawa Avenue
Howick
Auckland

Cimarron Lang
Cimarron Bears
136B Hanson Street
Newtown
Wellington

Frances McCleary
Braidwood Bears
RD 9
Frankton
Hamilton

South Africa

Mary Kelly
Bear Basics
The Railway Station
Simons Town
7995 Cape Town

Switzerland

Karin Koller
Pink Dino Bears
Emmentalstrasse 22
3510 Konolfingen

The United States

Gloria Franks
"By Goose Creek"
Rt. 1, Box 221 B
Walker, WV 26180

Elaine Fujita-Gamble
9510 2342nd SW
Edmonds, WA 98020

Susan Redstreake Geary
New Mexico Bear Paws
2 Trueman Court
Baltimore, MD 21244

Frances Harper
Apple of My Eye
233 Main Street
South Hampton, NH 05827

Mary Holdstad
Mary Holdstad and Friends
17831 145th Avenue, SE
Renton, WA 98058

Susan Horn
Susan Horn Bears
1963 McKinley
Ypsilanti, MI 48197

Kathleen Wallace
"Stier Bears"
2540 Pottstown Pike
Spring City, PA 19475

TEDDY BEAR MAGAZINES

Australia

Bear Facts Review
PO Box 503
Moss Vale
NSW 2577
Tel: 61 48 6781 338

England

Hugglets Teddy Bear
Magazine/Guide
PO Box 290
Brighton BN2 1DR
Tel: 01273 697974

Teddy Bear Times
Avalon Court, Star Road
Partridge Green
West Sussex RH13 8RY
Tel: 01403 711511

France

Teddy's Patch
Le Club des Amis de L'Ours
34 rue Lieu de Santé
76000 Rouen
Tel: 33 35 88 9600

Japan

Teddy Bear Post
Japan Teddy Bear Fan Club
2-3 Nangu-Cho
Ashiya-City
Hyogo 659

The United States

Teddy Bear and Friends
Cowles Magazines Inc.
6405 Flank Drive
Harrisburg
PA 17112

The Teddy Bear Review
PO Box 1239
Hanover
PA 17331

The Teddy Bear Times
3150 State Line Road
Cincinnati
North Bend
OH 45052

The Teddy Tribune
254 W. Sidney Street
St. Paul, MN 55107

TEDDY BEAR CLUBS

England

British Teddy Bear Association
PO Box 290, Brighton
East Sussex BN2 1DR
Tel: 01273 697974

Japan

Japan Teddy Bear Fan Club
2-3 Nangu-Cho
Ashiya-City
Hyogo 659
Tel: 81 797 23 5533

United States

B.E.A.R.
Bear Enthusiast's All-Round
Collectors Club
313 Glenoaks Blvd.
Glendale, CA 91207

Good Bears of the World
PO Box 13097
Toledo, OH 43613

Muffy Vanderbear Club
North American Bear
Company, Inc.
401 North Wabash,
Suite 500
Chicago, IL 60611

Steiff Club USA
225 Fifth Avenue
Suite 1033
New York, NY 10010

MANUFACTURERS

Britain

Colour Box Miniatures
Bronze Age Limited
Orchard Estate, Lauder
Berwickshire TD2 6RH
England

Dean's Rag Book
The Dean's Company (1903)
Pontypool
Gwent NP4 6YY
Wales

Merrythought Ltd.
Ironbridge, Telford
Shropshire TF8 7NJ
England

France

Thiennot SA
BP 6 rue du Stade
10220 Piney

Germany

J. Hermann Spielwaren GmbH
D-96450
Coburg-Cortendorf
Germany

Gebruder Hermann KG
Amlingstadter Strasse 9
Postfach 1207
D-8606 Hirschaid

Margarete Steiff GmbH
Postfach 1560
D-89530 Giengen/Brenz
Alleenstrasse

Canada

Ganz Brothers Toys
One Pearce Road
Woodbridge
Ontario L4L 3T2

The United States

Applause Inc
6101 Variel Avenue
PO Box 4183
Woodland Hills
California
91365-4183

Dakin Inc.
7000 Marina Blvd.
Brisbane, CA 94005

Gund
One Runyons Lane
Edison
NJ 08817

Mary Meyer Corporation
PO Box 275
Townsend
VT 05353

North American
Bear Company
401 North Wabash
Suite 500
Chicago, IL 60611

SHOPS AND STORES

England

The Mulberry Bush
9 George St.
Brighton BN2 1RH

Sue Pearson Antique
and Collectors Bears
13½ Prince Albert St.
The Lanes
Brighton
BN1 1HE

Teddy Bears of Witney
99 High St.
Witney
Oxfordshire OX8 6LY

Japan

Bruin's Bruin
10,13-10 Utsukushigaoka
Midori-ku, Yokohama
Kanagawa 225

The Netherlands

Teddy Bear's Picknick
Kolstverlorenpad 1b
3961 CJ Wijk bij Duurstede

The United States

The Bear Care Co.
Suite 957-F
505 S. Beverly Drive
Beverly Hills
CA 90212

Bears N Things
14191 Bacon Road
Albion, NY 14411

Bears N Wares
312 Bridge Street
New Cumberland
PA 17070

The Calico Teddy
22 East 24th Street
Baltimore
MD 21218

F.A.O. Schwarz
767 Fifth Avenue
New York
NY 10153-0199

Old Friends Antiques
Box 754
Sparks, MD 21152

Village Bears and Collectibles
5128 Ocean Blvd
Sarasota, FL 34242

MUSEUMS

Britain

The London Toy and Model
Museum, 21-23 Craven Hill
London W2 3EN, England

The Teddy Bear Museum
19 Greenhill Street
Stratford-upon-Avon,
Warwickshire, CV37 6LF
England

Teddy Melrose
The High Street, Melrose
Roxburghshire TED6 9PA
Scotland

Germany

Margarete Steiff Museum
Giengen (Brenz)

Switzerland

Spielzeugmusuem
Baselstrasse 34
CH-4125 Richen

The United States

Children's Museum
P O Box 3000, IN 46206

Teddy Bear Castle Museum
431 Broad Street
Nevada City, CA 95959

Teddy Bear Museum of Naples
2511 Pine Ridge Road
Naples FL 33942

MISCELLANEOUS

Libearty
The World Society for the
Protection of Animals
2 Langley Lane
London, SW8 1TJ, England

Calendar of Events

JANUARY

Dolls, Bears, Supplies & Collectibles Show & Sale, San Diego, California Tel: 619 436 3844

Doll & Teddy Bear Show Hudson, New Hampshire Tel: 603 434 7398

Teddy Bear, Doll and Antique Toy Show and Sale San Diego, California Tel: 619 434 7444

Teddy Bear Show and Sale, Mesa, Arizona Tel: 708 798 0290

FEBRUARY

Convention and All Teddy Bear Show and Sale Seattle, Washington Tel: 503 775 3324

Winter Teddy Bear Extravaganza Newport, Rhode Island Tel: 203 585 9940

The Winter Bear Fest Kensington Town Hall, London W8, England

MARCH

Bearly Spring Show Tampa, Florida Tel: 813 286 7032

Doll, Toy, Bear Show Lansing, Michigan Tel: 517 694 3663

Teddy Bear Affair Syracuse, New York Tel: 315 446 1657

Teddy Bear Extravaganza Northboro, Maine Tel: 508 393 0016

Japan Teddy Bear Festival Tokyo, Japan

APRIL

Annual Doll & Teddy Bear Show & Sale Sharon, Pennsylvania Tel: 814 226 2743

Annual Show and Sale Jamesburg, New Jersey Tel: 908 329 3779

Eastern States Doll, Toy and Teddy Bear Show, West Springfield, Massachusetts Tel: 203 758 3880

Teddy Bear Convention Auction, Show and Sale, Schaumburg, Illinois Tel: 708 798 0290

The London Bear Fair, Fairfield Halls, Croydon, Surrey, England

MAY

The Bear Show and Sale, San Mateo, California Tel: 916 989 9291

Doll and Teddy Bear Show and Sale, Portland, Oregon Tel: 503 775 3324

JUNE

Teddy Bear Festival, Show and Sale, Rochester, New York Tel: 716 263 2700

Teddy Bear Jubilee Overland Park, Kansas Tel: 913 677 3055

JULY

Annual Teddy Bear Show and Sale, San Jose, California Tel: 408 263 1026

Festival of Steiff, The Toy Store, Toledo, Ohio Tel: 419 473 9801

Australia's Premier Bear Affair Sydney Town Hall, Sydney N.S.W., Australia

AUGUST

Rocky Mountain Teddies Copper Mountain, Colorado Tel: 503 775 3324

Teddy Bear Convention Timonium, Maryland Tel: 410 544 4526

British Teddy Bear Festival Kensington Town Hall, Hornton St., London W8, England

SEPTEMBER

Premier Doll and Bear Show Huntington, New York Tel: 516 667 7538

OCTOBER

Dream Catchers Dolls and Bears Show and Sale Phoenix, Arizona Tel: 602 956 2264

Teddy Bear Auction, Show & Sale Schaumburg, Illinois Tel: 708 798 0290

Doll and Teddy Bear Collectors Show, Sydney Town Hall, Sydney, Australia

Japan Teddy Bear Festival, Kobe, Japan

NOVEMBER

Beary Merry Christmas Show Columbus, Ohio Tel: 614 861 3502

Eastern States Doll, Toy & Teddy Bear Show and Sale West Springfield, Massachusetts Tel: 203 758 3880

DECEMBER

Teddy Bear Show and Sale Daytona Beach, California Tel: 904 798 0290

The British Bear Fair, Hove Town Hall, Horton Road, Hove, Nr. Brighton, England

Toy Mania, Parc des Expositions, Port de Versailles, Paris, France

Index

KEY

Collection

BC — Brooks Collection
CB — Colour Box Miniatures
CSK — Christie's South Kensington
CT — Calico Teddy
DA — Dottie Ayers
DH — Dee Hockenberry
ES — Illustrations by EH Shepard copyright under the Berne Convention (p.148)
FAO — FAO Schwarz
FF — Françoise Flint
GH — Gebrüder Hermann
HGS — Harper General Store
HS — Hermann Speilwaren
IP — Ian Pout
JH — Joan Hanna
JSC — Jennie-Sharman Cox
KS — Collection Kiok Siem
MH — Mimi Hiscox
Mth — Merrythought
NPG — by Courtesy of the National Portrait Gallery, London (p.148)
NYPL — From the Collection of the Central Children's Room Donnell Library Center, The New York Public Library (p.148)
C&VP — Clive and Valerie Picken
PB — Peggy de Boy
PC — Private Collection
SI — Smithsonian Institute
SP — Sue Pearson
S&TK — Stan and Dottie Kennedy

pp.12, 151, 153, 154 TM Dottie Ayers

Photography

FW — Fred Weegenaar
GD — Geoff Dann (©De Agostini Editions)
MP — Michael Pearson (©De Agostini Editions)
DA — Dottie Ayers
MW — Matthew Ward (©De Agostini Editions)
KW — with permission of Kunstverlag Weingarten/Germany from R. und C. Pistorius: Die schönsten Teddys und
Tiere — von Steiff
LH — Louk Heimans (©De Agostini Editions)
DH — Dee Hockenberry
HS — Hermann Speilwaren
B — Bonhams
Mth — Merrythought
RM — Reproduced by Permission of Royal Mail
AO — Andrew Oldacre
MBP — Mike Brown Photography
FP — Flair Postcards

t top **b** bottom **r** right **l** left **c** center

While every effort has been made to credit every bear owner and photographer, and to trace the present copyright holders where relevant, we apologize in advance for any unintentional omission or error and will be pleased to insert the appropriate acknowledgment in any subsequent edition.

PICTURE CREDITS

1 SP/GD; 2 KS/FW; 6 SP/GD; 7 SP/MP; 8 tr SP/MP, c PC/MP, bl SP/MP, br DA/DA; 9 tr SP/MP, cCSK/MP, bl SP/MP, br CSK/MP; 10 l SP/MP, r PC/MP; 12 tr SI, tl SP/MP, cl PC/MP, cr DA/DA, bc CT/DA, br DA/DA; 13 tr SP/MP, cl&cr SP/MP, bl CSK/GD, br SP/MP; 14 tr DA/DA, bl SP/MP, cb SP/MW, br SP/MP; 15 tl CT/DA, tr JSC, bl SP/MP, br C&VP/MP; 18 SP/GD, 20 SP/GD; 21 tl SP/MP, br CSK/MW; 22 tl SP/MP, bPC/DA; 23 t KS/FW, bl KS/FW, crSP/MP; 24 t SP/MP, b SP/MW; 25 t SP/MW except 2nd left SP/MP, bl SP/MW, br SP/MP; 26 tl CSK/GD, tr CSK/CSK, bl KW; 27 CSK/GD; 28 tl SP/MW, b KS/FW; 29 SP/MP; 30 t KS/LH, b CSK/GD; 31 t PC, tr PC; b KS/LH; 32 t CSK/GD, b KS/LH; 33 t CSK/GD, bl SP/MW, c PC, c DH; 34 SP/MW; 35 KS/LH, except cr PC; 36 KS/LH; 37 tl KS/LH, tr SP/MP, bl KS/LH, bc KS/LH, br PC; 38 all KS/LH except tr SP/MP; 39 KS/LH; 40 t HS, b CSK MP; 41 HS; 42 tl CSK/MP, b CSK/GD; 43 tl CSK/MP, cl CSK/GD, cr CSK/GD, b CSK/MP; 44 tl PC, b CSK/GD; 45 tl KS/HL, tr KS/FW (inset PC), bl SP/MW, bc KS/LH, br CSK/MP; 46 tl SP/MP, bHGS/DA; 47 t PC, tc PC, c SP/MP (all), b SP/MP (all); 48 tl SP/MP, bl PC, br SP/MW; 49 SP/MP (all); 50 tl PC, bl CSK/GD, br CSK/GD; 51 tl B, tr PC/MP, c SP/MP, bl SP/MP, br CT/DA; 52 SP/GD; 53 tl SP/MP, br SP/MP; 54 tl SP/MP, b SP/MW; 55 tl SP/MP, tr SP/MP, bl SP/MW, c (both) SP/MP; 56 SP/MW; 57 tr SP/MW, all others SP/MP; 58 l (all) SP/MP, br CSK/GD; 59 t SP/MP (all except 2nd left CSK/MP); 60 tl SP/MP, b SP/MW; 61 Deans tl DH/MP, tc MC/MP, tr MC/MP; bl PC/MP, rc MC/MP; 62 tl SP/MP, tr SP/MP; 63 all MC/MP except br Deans; 64 tl SP/MP, b SP/MW; 65 t (all) SP/MP; b SP/MW; 66 t SP/MP, b CSK/GD; 67 tl SP/MP, tr SP/MP, bl CSK/GD, br CSK/GD; 68 tl SP/MW, b SP/MW; 69 t SP/MP (all), bl CSK/GD, br CSK/MP; 70 t PC/MP, bl CSK, br SP/MW; 71 t SP/MP (all), b Mth; 72 tlSP/MP, b SP/MP; 73 tl CSK/MP; tr (both) SP/MP, b SP/MP (all); 74 tl CSK/GD, tr (both) SP/MP, b CSK/MP; 75 tl SP/MP, tr SP/MP, b (both) CSK/GD; 76 tl SP/MP, br SP/MP; 77 tl SP/MP, tr SP/MP, b (all) SP/MP; 78 tl PC/MP, b SP/MW; 79 t SP/GD, c SP/MW, b SP/MP; 80 t PC/AO, c FW/MP, b CSK/GD; 81 t FW/MP, c SP/MP, b SP/MP; 82 tl PC/MBP, bl PC/MBP, br SP/MP; 83 tlJH/MBP, cl JH/MBP, cr PC/MBP, bl PC/MBP (both); 84 SP/GD; 85 SP/MP; 86 tl PC/MP, bl SP/MP, br PC/MP; 87 PC/MP (all); 88 CSK/GD; 89 PC/MP (all); 90 tl SP/MP, bl PC, br SP/MW; 91 PC/MP (all); 92 PC/MP (all); 93 t PC, b PC/MP, b PC/MP; 94 KS/FW; 95 SP/MP; 96 tl CT/DA. b SP/MP; 97 tl CT/DA, tc PC/DA, tr CT/DA, bl DA/DA, bc CT/DA, cr CT/DA; 98 t (l to r) Ct/DA, CT/DA, CT/DA, CT/DA, MH/DA, cl DA/DA, c CT/DA, B MH/DA; 99 (l to r) CT/DA, CT/DA, S&TK/DA; bl SP/MP, bc CT/DA, br PB/DA; 100 tl FF/DA, bl DA/DA, br PC/DA; 101 tl DA/DA, tr KS/FW, c DA/DA, bl MH/DA, brPC; 102 t MH/DA, c FF/DA, bl DA/DA, br DH; 103 tl CSK/GD, bl FF/DA, br CSK/GD; 104 tl SP/MP. bl PD/DA, br SP/MP; 105 t (l to r) FF/DA, PD/DA, FF/DA, FF/DA, bl SP/MP, bc CT/DA, br FF/DA; 106 t (all) S&DK/DA, bl SP/MP; 107 l CT/DA, c CT/DA, r S&DK/DA; 108 tl DA/DA, Deag/MP; 109 l CT/DA, tc (both) PD/DA, bl PD/DA, br CT/DA; 110 FAO/MP; 111 t CT/DA, c PD/DA, bl PD/DA, br CT/DA; 112 SP/GD; 113 BC; 114 BC except br FW/MP; 115 BC; 116 BC; 117 BC; 118 tl DA/DA, bl CSK/GD; 119 tl DA/DA, tc DA/DA, tr SP/MP, b (l to r) DA/DA, CSK/MP, CSK/MP; 120 tl PC/MP, bl MrP/MP, br SP/MP; 121 t (both) GH, bl SP/MP, bc IP, br SP/MP, tr KS/LH; 122 tl PC/MP, tr CSK/GD, b (all) SP/MP; 123 l SP/MW, t CSK/GD; 124 SP/GD; 126–141 PC, except 133 bl PC/MP; 142 tl SP/MP, bl SP/MP, br SP/FP; 143 tr CB, bl CSK/GD, br CSK/GD; 144 tl SP/MP, tr PC, b SP/MP; 145 t SP/MP, b SP/MP; 146 t PC; b MrP/MP; 147 t Mth; b SP/MP, rc DH/MP; 148 tl ES tr NPG; bl NYPL, cr DA/DA; 149 t (l to r) DA/DA, CSK/GD, DA/DA, bl SP/MW; 150–151 From the Collection of Dottie Ayers; 152 tl CT/DA, bl CT/DA, br SP/MP; 153 t to b CT/DA, CT/DA, CT/DA, DA/DA; 154 t SP & DA, bl CSK, br CSK; 155 t, bl CT/DA, cr DA/DA; tr RM, bl CT/DA, br DA/DA; 156 SP/MP (all); 157 tc SP/MP, tr FF/DA, bl SP/MP, c SP/MP, bc CSK/MP, br SP/MP; 158 t SP/MP, b SP/MP; 159 bl CSK/GD, c SP/MP, ct SP/MP, br SP/MP; 160 SP/GD, 162 tl SP/MP, bl SP/MP, br CSK/GD; 163 t CSK/GD, c SP/MP, b SP/MP; 164–165 SP/MP (all); 166–167 SP/MP (all); 168 tl MD/MP, bPC/MP, bl PC; br SP/MP; 169 t PC, cl PC, cr MD/MP, bl SP/MP, br SP/MP; 170 tl SP/MP, b SP/MP; 171 SP/MP (all)

Editor Alison Macfarlane
Designer Manisha Patel
Editorial Assistant Philippa Cooper
U.S. Editor Mary Ann Lynch

Publishing Director Frances Gertler
Art Director Tim Foster
Reprographics Manager David Blundell
U.S. Consultant Erica Marcus

Indexer Christina Shuttleworth
Image Processors Edward Jackson, Jonathon Drury

Authors' acknowledgments

We wish to thank all our dear friends without whose help this book would not have been possible, especially Marcelle Goffin and Teddy's Patch, Le Club des Amis de L'Ours, Han and Kiok Siem, David Douglas, Jackie and Mike Brooks, Leyla Maniera and the teddy bear department at Christie's South Kensington and Michael Crane of Dean's. We would also like to thank Joan Hanna, Dr. Ursula Hermann at Hermann-Spielwaren, Mrs. G. Lee at Gebruder Hermann, and Oliver Holmes at Merrythought, for the pictures and information they have provided us with. Also Jill and Dermott Palmer Antiques in Brighton, for the kind loan of their props, Mr. Punch toyshop in Brighton, Ruth Bowman who helped keep Sue's shop running when she was busy working on the book, Geoff Dann, Matthew Ward, and Michael Pearson for taking lovely photographs of the bears, and last but not least Alison Macfarlane and Manisha Patel whose help and hard work we couldn't have done without.